D0104683

The Spirits Around Us

Michael H. Brown

Spirit Daily Publishing
www.spiritdaily.com
11 Walter Place
Palm Coast, Florida 32164

The Spirits Around Us by Michael H. Brown

Copyright © 2010 Michael H. Brown

Published by Spirit Daily Publishing

For additional copies, write:
Spirit Daily Publishing
11 Walter Place
Palm Coast, Florida 32164

or contact: www.spiritdaily.com

ISBN 978-0-615-39724-5

Printed in the United States of America   First Edition

For all I have known who are on the other side,
particularly my grandparents on both sides, my
godparents, Gramma McVinnie, Uncle Pete, Uncle Sam,
Uncle Tony, Russell, and Jonathan

Chapter 1

There are angels. There are demons. There are souls of the deceased. There are spirits all around, and they influence us—and everyone *around* us—far more than we usually reckon.

They nudge. They send signs. Mainly, we *feel* them. Sometimes, they materialize in dreams. At fleeting moments, we may even get a glimpse of them. They warn. They affect our moods. They have been responsible for inspiring us. They have been responsible for distress. On the other hand, they have been responsible for elation. They have brought you together. They have pulled you apart. They have deceived. They have helped you—the good ones—while others have attacked, creating tension.

Some have healed, while those that are evil may even have caused illness.

Some latch onto us. Some (perhaps, for your discernment) have been with our families for generations.

Perhaps, they affect us mentally, emotionally, spiritually, and physically.

It is the spiritual dynamic around us and it is not to be superstitious but to realize how spirits can be influencing our lives, how we are susceptible to them, and how we can free ourselves (and families).

We all have heard of the angels: There is the guardian, who has watched over you since conception. This angel should be invoked and thanked each day. When you die and look back (beyond the "veil"), you will be astonished at the interactions.

Some folks have more than one. It depends on what we are going through as well as our "mission."

Countless times in your life, you have been helped or even saved by this guardian, without knowing it. There are angels that serve as additional guardians or come at particular times or (as in the case of the great one, Michael) if you have invoked them. Focus on these spirits.

Their counterparts, of course, are demons—evil or "dark" spirits that afflict us (usually without our knowing, and sometimes, severely). It is not our job to energize them (which happens when we focus on them too much)—but to recognize where they are in order to extirpate them.

Throughout our lives, events and circumstances as well as meetings that are negative can be orchestrated by evil spirits, in the same way that angels orchestrate positive events. They are the "polar opposite" of light, and they are prevalent in our time. We must cast them out, as Jesus instructed, at every opportunity.

Then there are spirits of the departed.

Here we have to be extra cautious. Here, we need special discernment. Here, we look at passages from Scripture such as *Luke* 24:39 (when Jesus says "a ghost does not have flesh and bones") and *Job* 4:15 (when "a spirit passed by my face; the hair of my flesh bristled up"—which may have been a "ghost," a demon, or an angel, for all we know). We do know from *2 Maccabees* 15:12-16—as I shall repeat later—that the prophet Jeremiah appeared to a Jewish leader in a dream.

As one writer, Brother Ignatius Mary, put it, there are certain things about spirits we can draw from Scripture. That they do not have physical bodies—flesh and bones—we can take from *Luke* 24:39. That they can communicate with the living can be seen in *Sirach* 46:20 or *1 Samuel* 28. We know that "at least in some context allowed by God," the dead can be raised (*1 Samuel* 28). The Bible also tells us it's possible for "the dead to appear on the earth" (*Matthew* 72; *1 Samuel* 28). Likewise, it may be possible for the dead to not only to manifest on the earth, "but appear to people and talk with them" (*Luke* 16:27-31; 1 *Samuel* 28). "We know that it is possible for the living to bi-locate (*Revelation* 17:3; 21:10; *Corinthians* 12:2)," argues this writer. "We know that it is possible for spirits to communicate in dreams and the person to have a bodily reaction to the visitation (*Job* 4:15)."

It was the opinion of Father F. X. Schouppe, who wrote the famous *Purgatory: Explained by the Lives and Legends of the Saints*, that "the spirits of the dead sometimes appear to the living" and that this is "a fact that cannot be denied. Apparitions of the souls that are in purgatory are a frequent occurrence. We find them in the 'Lives of the Saints'; they happen sometimes to the ordinary faithful."

He quotes St. Thomas Aquinas as saying, "A very probable opinion and one which, moreover, corresponds with the words of the saints in particular revelation is, that purgatory has a double place for expiation. The first will be destined for the generality of souls, and is situated below, near to hell; the second will be for particular cases, and it is from thence that so many apparitions occur."

Also, through the centuries are the claims of souls appearing from Heaven.

This is a topic that few in the Catholic realm—or any Christian denomination—tackle: spiritual forces that are neither angelic *nor* demonic but represent those who once lived on the earth. It must be approached with great caution because there can be great deception (or imagining). While the Church does not outright reject the notion of disincarnate or disembodied spirits (as they are also called), neither does it categorically accept them.

We must respect those who interpret Church statements as arguing against such spirits, as well as maintain a guard against those of a New Age or even occult slant who delve into this realm, which presents danger.

Because Satan can so easily fool our senses, notes the first writer I quoted, we are well advised to look upon all ghostly events with great skepticism as to the idea of whether they come from God. "First we must recognize the great possibility that we are imagining things," noted Brother Ignatius. "The human mind has great imagination capacity and we can psyche ourselves into seeing things that are not there or to misinterpret optical illusions. Second, we must always presume that we may be tricked by Satan and what we are seeing is a demon in disguise or Satan taking advantage of our overactive imaginations or optical illusions. A Godly apparition will never contradict any public revelation. A Godly apparition will never lead you to disobey your elders, superiors, or the Church (so we need to be aware of Church teaching and the like). Although meeting a spirit is scary, a Godly apparition will lead you to peace. A Godly spirit will always and without question affirm the Lordship of Jesus Christ. Thus we need to test the spirit with the formula of *1 John* 4:1-3."

I believe that when they are around, deceased spirits can have a great effect on us—positively *or* negatively.

In this realm are souls that may have gone to the other side, but who may manifest at particular times for particular reasons. They may be in purgatory or Heaven and appear to us in dreams and through "signs": objects that appear or seem to disappear, coincidences, and in some cases, apparitions. Included in this class would be saints and other figures of holiness, especially the Virgin Mother, who is at the highest level.

Among the deceased are also "earthbound" spirits—souls that many claim still roam the earth. This may be an area of special trouble. Some priests believe that, largely unrecognized, such spirits may cause many effects among the living. Once again, it is unwise to become overly intrigued but equally unwise to ignore their existence.

After realizing what they are, and what they can do (if this is our discernment), we move on to deliverance.

They may be included among those Jesus referred to as "unclean" spirits. Neither heavenly nor demonic, they can also be viewed as caught in a "void" (between here and the eternal). It was said that St. Padre Pio saw more spirits of the dead than humans who were alive (and prayed these spirits toward the embrace of Heaven—to the Light of Jesus).

The point is that we are surrounded by an invisible, dynamic world—one that is treacherous or glorious, alarming or beckoning, and thus must orient us to proper devotion and prayer and love. It is not a realm that should be tackled by thrill-seekers. It is certainly not a realm that should be approached with an Ouija board, medium, or ghost-hunters. This is supremely hazardous. Indeed, as Scripture warns, "There shall not be found among you any one that maketh his son or his daughter to pass through the fire, or that useth divination, or an observer of times, or an enchanter, or a witch. Or a charmer, or a consulter with familiar spirits, or a wizard, or a necromancer" (*Deuteronomy* 18:10-11).

That is the underside of an awesome truth, and that truth is that we live forever.

Right now, we are on a temporary journey. Our planet is like a testing ground or school where we learn and are purified. (If not, we are purified after.)

An objective look at near-death experiences can lead to no conclusion other than the spirit transcends the physical body and on death moves to another dimension.

As one doctor, Dr. Jeffrey Long, of Louisiana, who has extensively studied those who "died" and returned, says: "Millions of near-death experiencers happen worldwide every year to people who are unconscious and may be clinically dead with a loss of breathing and heartbeat. Yet they are still having lucid experiences at the time of death, experiences that are clear, logical, and well structured. By studying thousands of detailed accounts of near-death experiencers, I found the evidence that led to this astounding conclusion: near-death experiences provide such powerful scientific evidence that it is reasonable to accept the existence of an afterlife. Yes, you read that correctly. I have studied thousands of near-death experiences. I have carefully considered the evidence near-death experiences present regarding the existence of an afterlife. I believe without a shadow of a doubt that there is life after physical death."

As believers in Jesus, we need no such "proof." To go through the many trials of life and maintain love for God is what counts—above everything. Blind faith, they call it. Live by faith. And love. Unconditional love. Remember those two words.

But glimpses of the other side provide valuable insights about the spiritual world, including deceased loved ones and the unseen world around us.

Often, in our lives, we sense the presence of close relatives, and indeed, they often affect us.

Mothers, fathers, brothers, sisters, wives, husbands, daughters, sons. Friends. Long-lost aunts. Great-great grandparents. One child who lost consciousness during a near-death brush drew the portrait of a girl she met on the other side. When her parents saw it, they turned "ashen." It was a deceased sister who had died long before the girl was born and had been unknown to her. Dr. Long writes that during clinical death "encounters with the deceased loved ones are almost always joyous reunions, not horrifying ones like what might be seen in a ghost movie. Also, although many deceased loved ones prior to death were elderly and sometimes disfigured by arthritis or other chronic illnesses, the deceased in the near-death experience are virtually always the picture of perfect health and may appear younger—even decades younger—than they did at the time of death. Those who died as very young children may appear older. But even if the deceased appear to be a very different age than when they died, the [person] still recognizes them."

The point is that the spirit does not lapse into sleep nor dissolve when the body ceases to function.

Those who "die" and return say that in fact they felt more alive (and aware) than ever. They try to depict what they saw as a new reality with unusual flora, living waters, strange luminous buildings, streets of crystal, glowing streams, and colors that make the brightest and most beautiful ones on earth look like naught more than a photographic negative.

Always, there is the depiction of great light.

And it is around us even here on earth.

The other dimensions intersect with ours.

In a normal state, however, we can't see them.

We may be granted snippets during dreams (when the mind seems to roam from its physical roost), or in those brushes with the eternal, or by way of mystical experiences (including those of saints). But it is impossible for us to grasp the full reality of Heaven (which will take eternity to explore). It was after such an experience that a famous theologian named St. Thomas Aquinas permanently stopped all of his writing, describing it as "straw" in comparison with the truth of the Light he had observed.

Meanwhile, St. Paul discussed a man who left his body and saw a level of Heaven (*2 Corinthians* 12:2-4).

St. Augustine recounted the story of a haunted house (City of God, Book XXII, chapter eight).

Thomas Merton encountered the apparition of a deceased sister.

Bishops have reported apparitions. So have priests. Too often, modern theology discounts it.

You will be astonished at some of the accounts.

For the supernatural weaves in and out of all of our lives and in some fashion everyone has had a glimpse (if they think long enough about it).

Knowing we live beyond the grave, what could depress us? What should stop us? Does not even the worst "tragedy" pale in comparison to the reality of eternity and reunification with all whom we have loved?

We are, above all, spiritual beings. We have a spiritual essence. We also have spiritual antennae.

When it is properly tuned, through Jesus, through prayer, it begins to organize such experiences into an approach to a reality that is forever.

Chapter 2

When a person dies, he is supposed to go to Jesus. According to mystics, the soul is often granted a choice between doing this immediately or after the funeral (in order to assist those who grieve). This is why there are often "signs" at wakes, the funeral Mass, or at the cemetery. Few know that when Pope Paul VI passed on August 6, 1978, his Polish alarm clock rang the moment he died (and in October that year, of course, a Polish Pope took over in Rome).

Other signs may include the sudden, unusual appearance of an object or the way the sun shines through a cloud.

One Catholic woman who claims supersensory capabilities asserts that since childhood she has witnessed how the deceased seem to stand near their caskets, watching as loved ones file by, aware of everything that is said or done. When there are commemorations, the presence may be stronger.

Years after a person dies, he or she may "appear" to a loved one in a vision, dream, or manifest through unlikely events. When a soul is from Heaven, his or her presence is filled with light, happiness, and peace. He is luminous. There may even be an "aroma of sanctity" (the fragrance of roses and lilies but better). Often, the deceased will appear as he or she was at his or her prime, between 25 and 35 years in age, clear-eyed, and fit, with a sense of love, fullness, and well-being, in a fashion of dress that will identify him to the person he is visiting—perhaps a suit, dress, or uniform. If the soul is in Heaven, the attire may also be a splendid white robe or some other radiant color (like a combination of spun glass and spun cotton).

If of God, the residual feeling is positive.

If there is fear, it can be a warning signal.

If a spirit comes around too often, it should be prayed into the Light of Jesus.

In fact, this prayer should be said for all souls.

Of course, we also experience fear when we confront the unknown—good *or* evil. The apostles were afraid when they saw Jesus walking on water. The presence of a spirit is often accompanied by that tingling feeling on our skin or the sensation of being watched.

Often such manifestations are to help us, seek our assistance, or warn (when they are from those we loved).

In other cases, the deceased may be around because they are somehow trapped—afraid to enter God's Light, confused by their death, unable to forgive themselves, or overly attached to the world.

For when we die, we die into our real selves. We die into who we really are. We go to that level to which we had advanced (or digressed). Our personalities remain with imperfections. There is Heaven, hell, and purgatory. I have written of this before.

Souls from purgatory are often around us—and need prayer.

In purgatory, according to some Catholic mystics, the soul cannot pray for itself and in the lower levels may not even immediately benefit from the prayers of others.

At the *lowest* level, purgatory may be much like hell: a darkness so dense it's nearly palpable.

There may be extremes of cold and hot, even fire (though it is different from hell in that the souls at these lowest levels know that one day they will get out; they are "saved").

A soul in purgatory wears a robe that's "stained" or gray in proportion to transgressions for which it atones.

Such a soul may appear to the living looking doleful or at least serious. They manifest in a way that expresses their suffering. In Rome is a museum with artifacts from souls who left burn marks (including hand imprints on wood).

Instead of being seen, groans may be heard or there may be disturbances in a home.

Below purgatory, of course, is hell, and by some reckonings, souls from here too can sometimes pay a visit on the living—a decidedly unwelcome event. For a condemned soul is devoid of goodwill and love (one would surmise), searching for nothing other than to hurt someone living (this may be its only "joy"). Some "visionaries" have seen hell as a fire into which people enter and are transformed into awful, demon-like entities. In one description, a beautiful young woman was seen entering the "flames" and then coming out as a creature that was half beast and half human—a classic depiction of an evil spirit, opening the question of whether condemned souls join fallen angels (as demons).

One former atheist who had such an encounter said he found himself in a foggy place with "former humans" who looked like people with sharp bicuspid teeth and fingernails and insulted and ridiculed him and tried to tear at his spiritual flesh.

We need not dwell on this.

As we venture into these cases, it is crucial to know what we ourselves must do to avoid such a fate and achieve freedom in God and eternity. The goal of unconditional love for God and every person should be our chief aim. This brings us the quickest entry into Heaven (or higher purgatory).

We must be humble. Humility is a shield of protection. The humble person finds less resistance. We must shake ourselves of "over-attachments." We must not overly cling to people, money, jobs, objects, homes, or past hurts, lest they delay our rise to the Lord. Cling only to Him. Go through your life and send love to everyone you should have loved and forgive every person every single slight or insult or harm. We must also forgive ourselves. If we die with guilt, we infringe upon the passing. Cling only to God.

Such special insights occur right around death and seem orchestrated by the spirits around us.

A doctor named John Lerma who worked for the hospice at the Medical Center of Houston and interviewed more than two thousand terminally ill wrote that, "At my core, I am a scientist, and I did not come to the idea of angels and non-physical entities easily. I believed science had not done enough to narrowly define life, so I began with a skeptical view of the seemingly large number of supernatural occurrences that preceded death. When possible, I found a rational explanation and most often attributed the patients' visions to their advancing disease, medications, or a complete shutdown of the body systems. Nevertheless, the similarity and sheer number of stories, as well as some unexplainable phenomena, began to weigh heavily in favor of something else. In the last days of life, the terminally ill retreat within themselves as a way of preparing to release their souls. They tend to relive events in the distant past with varying feelings and often need help in obtaining closure. During this time, the patient may stare intently at corners in the room, or have brief conversations with unseen spirits of deceased family members or brilliantly lit angelic beings. It is these spiritual beings that bring comfort and peace, and aid the patient in resolving unsettled emotional, interpersonal, and spiritual issues, with the ultimate goal of a peaceful transition to the afterlife."

How many of us have *not* seen or heard of loved ones who witness unusual things as they approach the "other side"?

Noted a woman named Sheila who wrote me: "My first husband died when he was not yet thirty-eight years old. He was angry and I wasn't sure whether he had made a good Confession when he had the Last Rites. Later, I remarried. Occasionally, I would see a mist-like figure move from my boys' bedroom to ours, and I would kid that it was just Dave checking on me. Then, sixteen years after his death, I had a dream and saw the figure crossing the hall again. I called out to it and more or less scolded it—saying that this had gone on long enough. 'Come out and reveal yourself.' The mist cleared and it was Dave. He said that he had just come to say goodbye. I told him I loved him and he said the same to me . . . Then he was gone. I never saw the 'mist' again. I believe he had not been ready to be with God due to his anger but finally had gotten beyond it."

Said another who wished to remain anonymous (as sometimes happens, for fear of ridicule): "My mother died over forty years ago, and shortly after she died, I had a very vivid and realistic dream about her. I don't usually remember any of my dreams for very long. This one I remember as though it happened yesterday. In my dream, I heard the phone ringing. I got up and went downstairs to answer it. Everything was realistic: the stairs I went down, and the kitchen where the phone was. I picked up the phone, said hello, and it was my mother, sounding happy (which she wasn't the last years of her life). She asked if I knew who it was, and I said yes. She told me that she had called me because she knew I was concerned about her (she had died an alcoholic). She said she felt much better and said she knew her behavior on earth was wrong. I seemed to hear voices in the background, and she said, 'Do you hear that? We're all busy here.' She then told me she was given only a little time to talk to me. I wanted her to talk longer, and she replied somewhat firmly that she couldn't. I asked her if she would call me again, and she said 'no'—that I would see her again some day, but not for a long time. She said, 'You have to raise your children.'"

We cannot dismiss this as solely a dream.

Recalled Jayni Flories of Las Vegas: "The week my mother was dying my sister and I took turns staying up nights with her.

"One night I thought I heard her sort of choking so I went to her bedside to see. She was sleeping peacefully. The door to the bedroom was open and out of the corner of my eye I could see sort of a figure standing in the hallway. I couldn't see a face, just the torso and hands folded in front. It appeared to me that the hands were those of a man. When I turned to look I couldn't see anything, but when I turned back to look at my mother I again saw the figure out of the corner of my eye.

"The next day when I told my brother and sister about it, they both very nonchalantly said, 'Oh, it's Daddy coming for Mom.' Our father died in 1966 and this was 1992. A few days later my mother died."

The pattern: a thin veil as folks are dying, and then just after they pass. Time and space are no obstacles.

"Thanksgiving weekend of 2007, while visiting my daughter in North Carolina, I woke up about two a.m. on a Sunday morning from a deep sleep to find myself 'in' my mom's hospital room in New Jersey!" wrote a viewer of our website named Diane Dodd who seemed to have a mystical encounter. "I was seated in the corner of her hospital room, along the wall where her head lay. I could sense Jesus and Mary standing on either side of Mom caressing her face [in this dream].

"*As I looked toward the open door*, I saw my grandmother come into Mom's hospital room with all the children that both my mom and I had miscarried. It was as if Jesus and Mary were inviting them to come to my mom! It was so peaceful, beyond any words I can describe. I could see the joy on my grandmother's face as she introduced all the children to my mother. Seeing Mom's room fill with such joy and happiness, where is the fear, one wonders, if this is what dying is like?

"The vision gave me such peace that I was able to go back to sleep.

"*Later that same Sunday* morning, my family arrived at church early so I could pray in the Eucharistic Chapel and immediately I was 'back' in my mother's room! Jesus and Mary were still on either side of her bed and I saw all my mother's relatives coming into the room to welcome her; some I did not recognize. Without taking their eyes off my mom, each told me who they were and how they were related to Mom.

"Finally, my grandfather (whom I had never met) peeked into the room. He left the family when my mom was only four years old. He was the only person I was actually able to have a conversation with and he 'said' that he could not come into the room until mom was actually gone. If he did, it would bring her great distress. It would only be when she was finally 'home' that she could fully forgive him for all he had done to her and the family, and it was not yet time for that. How blessed for me to see and experience my mother's near-death experience; to see her surrounded, welcomed, and supported in heavenly prayer made visible to my earthbound eyes! All of this gave me such peace and comfort, especially since I was so far away at the time. If we could only have eyes to see! As Our Lady says, the veil between earth and Heaven is so thin."

On the deathbed, angelic or deceased beings come to help review a person's life and ease the pain, unless pain is sent as a means of purification (turning soon to joy, as does redemptive suffering; many have insights into how suffering abets God's Plan).

Three to five days before death, says a doctor I previously quoted, "angels and deceased loved ones are present almost twenty-four hours a day."

The sooner relatives release their fears, anger, or abnormal attachments to the dying, the sooner the dying person will pass into the heavenly realm.

"Most patients who linger for weeks are often being kept on the earthly plane due to someone else's selfish reasons or, rarely, a patient's own deep-rooted and unresolved darkness," says another researcher in a book on the subject. "This applies to all people who love each other and are forced to part through death. It makes no appreciable difference whether it's a pair of lovers, a parent and a child, or two close friends. All partings hurt equally. Unfortunately we simply don't comprehend the consequences of our behavior. We don't know that through our great sorrow and despair we tie our beloved soul with great virtual chains thereby doing a great wrong—without mentioning the wrong we do ourselves. Grief and despair will not allow it to leave even though it has the right and the energy to do so, and at the appropriate time, too."

We all mourn. It is needed and natural. What causes problems is when—after a while—we refuse to let go, or reach into a state of despair, as opposed to simple sadness (or lonesomeness). We become "bound." One could note the classic depiction of ghosts rattling chains.

At times the "veil" or partition between here and here-after scrolls up like glass unfolding into itself, say those who have "died" and returned. They are very aware of what we are doing and saying. The Blessed Mother once told a visionary that when we pray for them, souls on the other side can see us. "I am not particularly 'holy,'" wrote Raven Wenner, a former Texan living in Cheshire, United Kingdom, "but for some reason God has allowed that I see people/things 'beyond the veil' since I was a child.

"When I was in my fifties I was an extraordinary minister of the Eucharist and used to take Our Lord to a devout housebound Catholic lady in her nineties.

"Despite being incredibly bent and wizened, she was 'all there'—though she slept most of the time.

"I sat with her one evening a week for over two years while her daughter, who was her sole caretaker, went out to dinner with her friends (caretakers badly need a break to keep from becoming depressed and ill themselves). I used to love being in the same room as this woman: her personal holiness was such that it felt the same as being in front of the Blessed Sacrament, full of peace and goodness.

"One night, just before dawn, I had a dream of a radiant young woman, tall, slim, and elegant in a dress of shimmering starlight coming toward me, smiling.

"She appeared and embraced me and even in the dream I felt a surge of joy and physical warmth radiate from her.

"She then turned and walked away into a beautiful landscape, and I awoke filled with wonderful happiness; the clock said five a.m.

"*At eight o'clock* the elderly lady's daughter called to say her mother had died peacefully—at five a.m. I realized she was the radiant beauty and had come to say 'thanks' for bringing Our Lord in the Eucharist to her, and sitting with her all those evenings.

"Until that time, I had looked at feeble, sick old age as a miserable fate; but now I realize that old age is but a temporary phase, in which many of us will come to interior perfection, as this woman did. I now am content with the idea of being old and ugly and poor and in pain—because if I live my Catholic Faith, old age is only temporary. I too will one day be like this lady, young and beautiful and full of joy in Christ forever. I see now that the trials and sicknesses and sorrows of old age are actually a merciful purgatory. It's much better to have it in this life than in the next like my other poor friend who drifted about haunting his brother's house as a ghost—until he had a Mass offered for him."

Indeed.

And shortly, we will encounter such cases.

Death is not to be feared, and we fear it only if we have not perfected love within us—for perfect love casts out all fear (and assures the subconscious that there is nothing to fear in eternity—which, with love, there isn't, since love gets us into Heaven).

"The mind without the heart leading," said one who had such an encounter, "is dangerous."

Through the sacraments, we have the opportunity for cleansing and finding the most direct way to a pleasant transition—and assisting those we love in doing the same.

We must realize that death is a great relief, the best thing—if we are attached to Jesus—that could happen to us, a free flight toward an incomprehensible, ecstatic domain.

Thus, fear and guilt must be released.

After Confession, guilt should be sent into the Wounds of Jesus.

Religion must lead to spirituality.

When it does, we are encompassed by bright spirits.

At their highest level, angels are "fiercely white," in the experience of the dying.

Phenomena may be attendant to such experiences.

When one priest died, the sky was seen to darken over the hospital, there were gale-force winds, and the lights flickered. A luminosity was seen to come from his body or bed, and feathers fell into the room—disappearing when the rain stopped and the lights came back on.

It was later learned that the priest collected feathers (in a bottle at his office).

We do not know and cannot know while on earth how these phenomena are coordinated. (When a fellow priest went to check the bottle, the feathers were missing.)

The spirit released from the body is no longer in the realm of physical laws.

Time and space evaporate. Often, a person who has a near-death experience can describe what was occurring at that time in other parts of the hospital or even to relatives at home miles away. They travel by merely thinking.

Can dark forces be present? Yes. It is not usually the case, but it is why we pray for the Blessed Mother's intercession "now and at the hour of our death."

The signs we are given!

"My sister-in-law was found dead in her apartment," wrote a viewer of our website named Carolina. "She lived alone and several hours away from us. She always told us that she would love to be buried in the old section of the cemetery where their parents were but always thought she would have to go over to the new part as there was no more room.

"As my husband and I struggled to arrange her funeral, we would find little clues among her belongings and we tried to meet her wishes to the best of our ability. As she had been dead a couple of days before she was found, it was necessary to have her cremated right away. When we approached the cemetery to arrange her internment, they advised that we would be able to bury her remains with her parents. We were overjoyed and knew that this would be exactly what she would have wanted! We had bought a large arrangement of roses with a statue of Our Lady of Grace in the center of it. As the funeral director was carrying the roses to the gravesite, one of the roses seemed to leap out of the arrangement and land at my feet. I was going to place it back in the arrangement but my daughter-in-law and the funeral director said, no, this is meant for you. I brought the rose home and placed it at the feet of our Sacred Heart statue, and it seemed like it would never dry out. There was such an overwhelming sense of peace."

"When I was 16, I fell off the back of a pickup truck in Griffin, Georgia," recalled another, Judy Duncan, of Ann Arbor, Michigan. "Now, down there the roads are very rough. Let's just say I was pretty messed up! While I lay there on the hot pavement with barely any clothes on, I remember such a feeling of peace it's too hard to describe. I also remember the people in my life who had passed on; it was as if they were standing in a group and I could hear, 'it's not time yet.' I looked at the trees around me and everything was glowing a very bright glow as if to say I did have life in me. It was awesome! While in the ambulance I was talking with a young girl (whom I assumed was the paramedic) and I remember her being so beautiful that I couldn't keep my eyes off of her.

It turns out there was no such paramedic.

"As I was sleeping in my hospital room I felt someone at the foot of my bed," continued Judy. "I don't know if it was a man or woman but he or she was glowing so bright the whole room lit up. This person specifically said to me as clear as day, 'Judy, do you know that God loves you?' I said 'yes' and fell right back to sleep. Of course, Mom insists to this day no one was in that room that night. But I'll never forget this experience as long as I live!"

Angels and the deceased manifest in many ways, especially when we are near death but throughout our lives, as is seen in so many testimonies of the departed. Often, says the Blessed Mother, they are looking for prayers. *"There are in purgatory souls who pray ardently to God, but for whom no relative or friend prays on earth,"* she was quoted as saying. *"It happens that God permits them to manifest themselves in different ways, close to their relatives on earth, in order to come close to God Who is just but good."*

"I thought I would add an experience I had with my father who passed away five years ago," wrote a viewer of our website, Shirley Bachmeier.

"I was on the treadmill listening to a beautiful instrumental [by a well-known Catholic musician] on his Glorious Mysteries CD. It was just lifting me into the heavenlies. All of a sudden I heard the voice of my father say to me, 'Shirley, I am learning how to love!' *The words just pierced through my mind and heart.* I nearly fell off the treadmill. What makes this so special is I never knew the love of my father. He did not know how to show his love while with us. In fact, he most often showed us the opposite of loving us.

"Just before he died, I was given the grace to forgive him and actually helped him to accept Jesus' forgiveness for his transgressions—so this was really a beautiful confirmation of his being in the place that was finishing the process of teaching him to love his family and being able to love us 'from the other side.' What a gift to all of us who were still struggling with his memories in our lives."

God's mercy is endless.

There is no one beyond it.

He forgives even mass murderers.

It only takes going to Him.

Otherwise, there is darkness.

Our angels will be there for us, as they are with us right now—every moment. They will seem so familiar that it will be as if we have known and loved them for eternities.

What about children who die before they're born?

"Many years ago when I was not practicing the faith, I had an abortion," is another note I received from a woman in Massachusetts. "Some years later, when I became a daily communicant, I spiritually baptized the child and gave the child a name.

"A few years passed and one early morning, I was lying in bed with a bad headache. Completely out of the blue and without warning, with my eyes closed, I saw the child's face! It was sort of glowing and looked to be about age five. The child was a boy and looked like other members of my family with sort of freckles around the nose.

"The child spoke and said, 'Mommy, I love you.'

"I remember reaching out—not physically, but in the vision-like state—and the child reached out to me.

"It lasted for a brief moment.

"I asked the child, 'Can you please stay?'

"At that point the vision faded."

Chapter 3

Often, the communications are nearly mischievous. Certainly, mysterious. But always leaving room for faith.

"In 2001, my mother-in-law Charlotte was diagnosed with stage-four colon cancer," said a man named Karl Mainig of Gilbert, Arizona. "She passed away on January 15, 2002—just a mere fifteen days passed her 66th birthday and two days before my wife Jennifer's birthday.

"Jennifer has a deep and profound love for her mother and when her mother passed she struggled and still does today. Also, my youngest son Zach was very close to his grandmother and was deeply affected by her passing.

"Christmas 2002, I decided to buy cell phones for my family—four in all, each family member having their own phone line," he explained. "The following January, the family was celebrating my wife's birthday. We had all just gathered to sing 'Happy Birthday' and eat cake.

"*After my wife blew out the candles,* she received a message on her phone. On the front screen of the flip phone a message read 'To Jennifer' and there was a box image with a bow wrapped around it—resembling a gift box or present. When she opened her phone to see who sent the message, the screen was blank. *The phone had no record of the message.*

"We thought that maybe the cell phone carrier knew it was her birthday and sent her the message, but we couldn't figure out how they knew which phone to send the message to (they were all registered in my name and there was no way they would have known what number was given to each family member). A month later, we were celebrating my son Zachary's birthday and in the same scenario, family and friends gathered to sing and have cake, and my son received a message on his phone identical to the one my wife received, reading 'To Zach' and the image of the gift box. When checking to see who sent the message, again there was no record of who sent the message!

"After researching a bit further, we found there was no functionality in the phone to create this type of message and send it to another individual and when talking to the phone carrier, they had no explanation. We all came to the same conclusion that it was my mother-in-law letting both my wife and Zach know that she was watching over them (and there to celebrate their special day)."

Recounted Michael Ziegler, who lost a daughter—and wondered if she was roaming a netherworld alone:

"In the early morning hours of March 17, 1984, around three a.m., I received an answer. All I can say was that I was taken to the place where people go after death. It was the most beautiful place I had ever seen. *Green hills as far as the eye could see* and a light in the sky but no source, like a sun or moon. Off to the right in a group of trees I could see a cloud that seemed to be filled with fire and was producing a sound of distant thunder. Then it happened! I heard my daughter call to me. I knelt down and I could see her clearly with her head and hands and her body appeared to be a spirit form in a type of green light. I carried her in my arms.

I said 'Vicky why are you here?' She said: 'I came to see you, because I know how much you love me Daddy.'"

The spirit world is all around us but it is a test of life that we cannot see or feel it the vast majority of time (for we are called to walk in faith).

After Hurricane Katrina, a woman named Valerie wrote to me about how she could feel her mother's presence "surrounding us" as they tried to patch up her home.

When the deceased are seen, this light engulfing them is sometimes like that around angels. This light, as we will see, depends on their level of purity. I have described beings in Heaven, hell, and purgatory in previous books. What we need here is to understand how they interact with us here on earth. It does seem plain that there are the angels, saints, Heavenly relatives, the dead in purgatory, and those dead who are "earthbound." An earthbound spirit is one that may be bewildered: for example, the soul of a non-believer or victim of violence who may not understand that death has occurred and is stuck pondering how he or she could still be conscious and yet without a physical body. This may be the mercy of the Lord allowing a soul to get its bearing, or even to purify, for eventually all souls must go to His Light, in which the truth of every life is shown with that same exquisite mercy.

A doctor in Moscow named George Rodonaia who was "killed" when he was struck by a car was confused when he found himself in a place of great blackness (still able to think but without a physical existence).

A person gets "stuck" if he is obsessed with antagonisms, traumas, material possessions, or people who are still on earth.

It is why Our Savior told us not to be attached to any thing or creature.

There are over-attachments to homes, to jewelry, to cars, to neighborhoods (a soul may roam from house to house). In a way, we "choose" where we begin our eternity. The soul gravitates to where it's most comfortable. If it's pure, it is comfortable in Heaven. If sullied, it needs purgatory. Some explain the place between here and eternity as a "void" while in other cases it seems to be what I have just said: a halfway place where there is no movement upward. In my opinion, *there are souls who will not leave the physical world.* When the Light comes for them, they chose not to enter it.

This makes it imperative, when we sense a spirit around, to pray that spirit into God's Light (in the Name of Christ).

Once more, it was because they are terrified at the prospect of a different dimension, afraid to review their lives with the Lord (or His angels), do not know they are dead, want to right a wrong, are bound to the despair of those who won't release them, do not believe they can be forgiven, or simply want to stay where they were. These souls are very important to recognize because they are virtually never discussed by the Church and can affect us in many ways.

Their actions are often confused with those of evil spirits or angels.

Here I note that Christ mentioned both demons *and* ghosts, which I will call "revenants."

Let's look at those mentions.

"When the disciples saw him walking on the lake, they were terrified. 'It's a ghost,' they said, and cried out in fear (*Matthew* 14:16).

"They were startled and frightened, thinking they saw a ghost," was the way *Luke* 24:37 put it.

"Look at My hands and my feet. It is I myself! Touch me and see; a ghost does not have flesh and bones, as you see I have," said Jesus (*Matthew* 24:39).

He would not have mentioned "ghost" if ghosts did not exist and His disciples would not have feared such entities if they didn't think such entities could cause damage.

If you want to get more explicit, look to *Isaiah* 19:3, where it says, "Then the spirit of the Egyptians will be demoralized within them; and I will confound their strategy, so that they will resort to idols and ghosts of the dead and to mediums and spiritists."

The Bible strongly indicates that ghosts (see King Saul) are real but also—as I have stressed—that we are not to initiate contact with them.

Noted an eminent Church scholar named Sir Shane Leslie long ago, "The Church forbids the dead to be evoked, but there is nothing to forbid the dead making the gesture themselves, since it is clear that only by Divine permission could they do so. Whether ghosts are miracles or not, Saint Thomas Aquinas accepts the apparition of the dead which he attributes to the special dispensation of God or else to the operation of spirits, good or bad."

Saint Gennadius once rebuked a specter that addressed him.

St. Eulogius of Alexandria saw a wraith.

Saint Amatus appeared after his death to his mother.

Saint Gregory tells of a deacon who haunted certain baths (and was seen by a bishop).

It is in his *Dialogues*.

In fact, many cardinals, bishops, priests, and nuns have been witness to apparitions or other "ghostly" happenings. By the year 1000, says another, Andrew Coynes, "stories of restless spirits of the departed, of ghostly violations of the traditional boundaries between the living and the dead, began to be recorded even by eminent churchmen."

The Church requires "no motion of faith for or against ghosts," is the way Sir Leslie (a consultant to Pope Pius XI) put it. In *City of God* (Book XXII), Saint Augustine mentions a haunted house—whether by an earthbound spirit or a demon, we cannot know—although an exorcism was performed, and perhaps there was no distinction for Augustine between the demonic and the earthbound (for elsewhere he seems skeptical of ghosts).

In the early Church, they were referred to as revenants, and there has been an explosion of reports in our own time.

"I don't know if I built my home on haunted property ten years ago, or if I am being visited by the holy souls," a woman named Dee Dee from Michigan wrote. "I only know that many nights when I lay in bed to read before falling asleep, I have encountered knocking on my wall above my bed in several places and that it does not cease until I pray. One night I was so unnerved that I pulled my Scapular out of my nightgown, made the Sign of the Cross, and kissed it. The knocking stopped right away. It's almost as if they were saying, 'can you put in a few good words for me?' While the sudden noises, occasional shadows, and missing objects at times startle me, I just say aloud, 'I will pray for you.' I believe that's the best way to handle a haunting. These souls are still on their journey and we must help them any way we can. I am very devoted to the Holy Souls."

Many such souls, it seems, are purgatorial. "In August of 2000 my dad passed away from lung cancer in Edmonton, Canada," wrote an engineering technologist named Waldo W. Ponce. "A few days later he came to me in a dream. He looked younger but serious and he was wearing a long white robe and said to me in Spanish, 'Tell [my brother] Ivan that purgatory exists. I was there for sixty-three days.' He then disappeared. The following morning for some reason I looked at a calendar first thing and counted sixty-three days from the death of my father and it ended on my brother Ivan's birthday."

Our prayers for them work—freeing them to Heaven.

"During the year of the Jubilee of John Paul II, when one could gain a plenary indulgence for a holy soul, my sister called from out of state and told me she was compelled to do the indulgence for my husband's mother, and that she would be completing the requirement for the indulgence the next day," said Jennifer Spillet. "I wanted to tell my husband about this when he arrived home from work that evening but completely forgot about it.

"The next day after he had arrived at work he called and said, 'I just had the strangest thing happen to me that I have ever had happen.' His voice was shaky but full of joy. Tearful.

"He proceeded to tell me that his mother went to Heaven that day.

"I asked what he was talking about. He said that on the way to work he was at a light waiting for it to turn green when the most beautiful music began playing (he didn't have his radio on) and an overwhelming feeling came on him of his mother's presence, that she was letting him know that she had gone to Heaven that day! I suddenly remembered my sister was completing her requirements for the indulgence that very day. I told my husband about my sister offering up the indulgence for his mother and after I hung up I called my sister and yes, you guessed it: she had finished her indulgence at about the same time this had happened to my husband!"

Said another named Karen Dembia: "I am a mother of four boys, ages one to ten. I have tried unsuccessfully to initiate the family Rosary off and on for years. My goal was one decade a night as a family. I heard that a novena said for the holy souls whom Our Lady most desires to deliver is incredibly efficacious.

"I began a novena asking the holy souls to please help my family commit to praying the Rosary together," Karen continued. "I told no one of my prayers. The next morning my eldest son, Anthony, told us of an incredibly vivid dream he had in which he was praying in a church with his eyes closed and when he opened them saw a parchment scroll with calligraphy that said, '*Dear Anthony, your family is destined for Heaven. You will go to Heaven one day too, but you will need to pray the Rosary every day, or you will be in purgatory for twenty years after your death. Love, Mary.*'

"He then saw the Blessed Mother as a living person.

"He described her hair, her veil, her dress, and so on. She smiled at him and then he woke up. When he had finished telling us this, my seven-year-old Kenny piped in and said, 'Well, we will all help you get into Heaven by praying the Rosary.' They remind me every night that we need to say the decade."

Chapter 4

It is said that we usually can't see spirits because they are at a different level in the same way we can't see television or radio waves. They are beyond the frequency of our normal spectrum. The greater the level, the higher the frequency (and the closer to Heaven). When the frequency is high enough (tremendous unconditional love), the only place the soul can "fit" is Heaven. This brings up the point that in a manner of speaking the soul, with Christ, "judges" itself and gravitates to where it feels most comfortable, which means where it best fits. It is love that most counts in attaining the higher places of the afterlife, which may be news to many who are judgmental and mean-spirited at the same time that they are meticulous in their religiosity. The coin falls into the proper slot. We go to the place we have created during earth (in another manner of speaking). After death, we find ourselves at the level that corresponds with our brightness or darkness. Selflessness purifies. So does suffering. Love covers a multitude of sins. Following death is a self-discovery, noted a mystic, in which the social masks worn on earth dissolve and the true self is revealed. If a soul was inwardly involved in goodness while on earth it will behave rationally. People who think about Divine matters while on earth are in touch with angels who will usher them into the afterlife. What a joy! "I am home. I am really home! *This* is my real home," will be the overwhelming emotion. It is a life of love and behaving honestly and fairly in every task that gets us to Heaven.

Souls at various levels interact with the living, some on missions from God—as sort of angels themselves—while others are confused or angry or trapped and in need of intercession.

Many cases come to us from nurses at hospitals—where of course so many make the passage.

"I used to work in an old Catholic hospital," noted one nurse on a major medical blogsite. "Where the labor and delivery unit is located now, it used to be the convent for the nuns that worked at this hospital.

"One of the nuns died of natural causes years ago. This nun loved and raised numerous varieties of roses. Ever since the obstetrics department was moved to this area, anytime a mother or baby is having difficulties you can smell the scent of roses throughout the whole unit.

"The obstetric nurses know to be prepared when they start smelling the scent. If a mother or baby dies, the room suddenly fills with rose petals. It is one of the creepiest but also most loving things that happen. I was standing in a room one night when the baby died. The room filled with white and pink rose petals. The rose petals just started floating down from the ceiling. It was like someone was just showering the room with them. This has happened several times over the years. I worked at another hospital where you would see a nurse in the old white dress and cap walk down the hallway and smile at you. Then she would walk into a patient's room and apply wrist restraints. All the nurses knew her. It was just Mildred who died sixty years ago. You had to follow her so you could take the wrist restraints off."

"We have had numerous reports from patients that they have seen a little boy," noted another nurse of a similar situation. "This boy comes in their rooms, turns their call lights on and off and throws things on the floor. The facility used to be an orphanage! Also, there are stories of an old-fashioned nurse in white dress and hat who would be seen going down the hall late at night doing her bed check and into someone's room and stay there for a couple minutes if they were really sick or about to die."

"I used to work in an old labor and delivery unit," is another account. "It was a small hospital, so often times I was back there by myself. I liked to keep the lights low and things quiet back there, so naturally I heard a lot of creaks and groans.

"There was a whole unused back hall; there was also no access to it except by passing me. I could hear metal objects clanging, and doors shutting—like somebody was getting ready for a C-section.

"I could always sense something there with me (it seemed).

"There was also a back room on the med-surg floor that was never used. It was a patient room converted to a storage room and that room was strange: call light always going off, and nobody near it. The whole hospital had a creepy aura. Maybe it was the cemetery next door."

Said a fourth: "We had a patient who was always on the call button. You know the type: the nurses have to take turns during the shift answering the call button so the primary can actually do other work. And this was a 'frequent flier' cause he was very chronic, very borderline, and the hospital was the only place he wouldn't fluid overload.

"I work seven p.m. to seven a.m. He died at about eight. The look on his face was like, 'how could you let me die!' Anyway, the family came and were gone by nine p.m. and he was gone to the funeral home at 9:30 p.m.

"At about 10 p.m., the call button started going off.

"I was there—call button going off every five minutes.

"One of the nurses was a very spiritual girl. At about two a.m., *after four hours of this*, she snapped, 'Enough!' She walked down to the room and practically screamed into the empty room, 'Mr. X, you have died. You can't be in here bothering us anymore. Move along. In the Name of Jesus, I'm exorcising you from this plane of existence. Go to the light and be happy!'

"And I kid you not: the call button stopped going off then and there."

Recalled a nurse named Timothy: "I worked in an intensive-care unit where a prisoner convicted of murder died in 'ICU 1'—and nobody would put a patient in that room after that because the air was too heavy and the room was too spooky and 'dark.' It was so bad that the hospital eventually closed down the room and knocked out a wall to make it a separate entrance into the unit. Nurses would refuse to put patients in the room even if it was the last available bed."

"My creepiest and scariest ghost story for me happened about a year ago," said yet one more health-care worker. "It really was more of a possession than a ghost story. I was helping another nurse with a patient who had lived a very hard life. There were numerous things going on with him, from cardiac to renal failure. You name it, he had it. This man was very afraid to die. Every time his heart monitor beeped, he would just go into a rage screaming, 'Don't let me die! Don't let me die!'

"The other nurse and I found out why he didn't want to die.

"About two a.m. his cardiac monitor started alarming.

"We both rushed into the room. I was pulling the crash cart behind me.

"When I got to the room, the other nurse is completely white. This man's whole look completely had changed. His eyes just had a look of pure evil on them and he had this evil smile on his face. He laughed at us and said, 'You stupid [curse word] aren't going to let me die are you?' He was sitting about two inches above the bed and was laughing."

"We were kind of frozen. I did reach up and hit the code-blue button and when I did the man went into ventricular fibrillation and crashed back onto the bed.

"We started 'coding' him, but after twenty minutes it was called off. Five minutes after the code was called, several of the code team was in the room cleaning up when this man sat straight up in the bed and said, 'You let him die. Too bad,' and then begins laughing. The man collapsed back to the bed. We heard a horrible, agonizing scream (actually every patient in the unit that night commented on the scream), and then you could hear 'don't let me die' being whispered throughout the unit.

"Every one of the nurses that night was pale and scared. Nobody went anywhere by themselves. By morning the whispers of 'don't let me die' were gone. The night shift nurses had a prayer service in the break room before we left for home and then we all had nightmares for weeks."

And also: "I don't know if this qualifies as a ghost story but here it is.

"I was taking care of a 12-year-old with aplastic anemia," posted a nurse on the website. "A week before she died, every day, at 12:15 p.m., I would get a cold chill across the back of my neck and the hair would stand up.

"I mentioned it to the evening nurse, who was convinced she [the patient] would die at that time.

"Several days later, her parents decided to cease all treatment. She lapsed into a coma. At twelve noon, she woke, asked me to hold her up, said goodbye to her parents, grandparents, and siblings. And died in my arms.

"It was 12:15 p.m."

Chapter 5

The supernatural is endlessly mysterious. There are knocks at night. There is rustling. Sometimes, there are voices; rarely, apparitions. There may be "orbs" of light—more than just the refraction (or digital functioning) of a lens. At other times, a spirit is actually *there*. Those with "gifts" say spirits are seen in greatest number where there are the greatest number of people, because spirits often attach themselves to living folks—making malls, airports, hotels, hospitals, and other densely inhabited (or trafficked) spots prone to the preternatural.

I myself have had a number of experiences in hotels.

In one case, I even had to change my room. In another, three of us heard sounds or felt a presence to the extent that we questioned the staff, who then confirmed that the hotel (in San Antonio) was "haunted" by the spirit of the owner's wife, who had killed herself there.

This is very common: that a spiritual occurrence will be attached to an untimely and especially to a violent death. We don't know why the spirit of a victim would hang around. Does it imply an inability to get beyond what occurred—or is it that the suddenness had caused consternation?

It all sounds bizarre and yet the accounts are *endless*. One poll showed that about half of Americans believe in ghosts and more than twenty percent believe they have seen or sensed such a presence.

That would extrapolate to about sixty million.

In Europe, there are so many haunted places that a list is not viable (see castles), and in fact the same is developing in the U.S.: every area has a list and these lists seem to be lengthening.

Famous "haunts" include Alcatraz; the battleground at Gettysburg; a penitentiary in Philadelphia; the Chelsea area of Manhattan; various spots in Savannah, Georgia (from restaurants to a motorcycle shop); the lighthouse in Saint Augustine, Florida; the Myrtles Plantation near Baton Rouge; the Hotel del Coronado in San Diego; the Stanley Hotel in Colorado (upon which a famous horror movie, *The Shining*, was based); and the Hollywood Roosevelt Hotel. In England, the Tower of London, once a prison (where beheadings took place, along with occult practices), is especially notorious.

Let's take a closer look at some of these.

For when we do, we notice a common thread: not only that a place has been around a while, but also that it was the scene of tragedy, materialism, or sinfulness. In some cases the deceased seem to be obsessed with the place while in others it appears that dark activity has wrought dark spirits.

Violence spins a soul into confusion.

We should not find titillation in such accounts but rather the occasion to pray for souls.

At the abandoned prison of Alcatraz in San Francisco are sounds of screams, slamming cell doors, and footsteps. Too many report it for us to dismiss it all as "superstition." At Gettysburg, many report ghostly apparitions of soldiers, sounds like cannon fire, and war cries, a website explains. The White House is filled with stories. As one encyclopedia notes, Abigail Adams's apparition has been spotted in the East Room, Dolley Madison is found lurking around the Rose Garden, Mamie Eisenhower's apparition is seen in the kitchen, and Abraham Lincoln's ghost has been seen in the Lincoln Bedroom. This was where Winston Churchill reportedly had an experience. During one of his visits to the United States during World War II, he retired late after relaxing in a long, hot bath (while drinking a Scotch and smoking a cigar) and couldn't believe his eyes when he climbed out of the bath, walked into the adjoining bedroom, and allegedly saw Lincoln standing by the fireplace in the room, leaning on the mantle.

The two men looked each other in the face, in seeming embarrassment, as Lincoln's apparition slowly faded away (Churchill was naked).

"Theodore Roosevelt, Herbert Hoover, Margaret Truman, Dwight Eisenhower, Jacqueline Kennedy, Ladybird Johnson, Susan Ford, and Maureen Reagan have all admitted sensing the presence of the Civil War president in the White House," says a site dedicated to such happenings. "Ladybird, wife of Lyndon Johnson, witnessed Lincoln's mysterious presence while she watched a television program about his assassination. She felt compelled to read a plaque above the fireplace, which explained the dead president's connection to the room. Gerald Ford's daughter, Susan, saw Lincoln's ghost in the room in the 1980s. In 1987, Ronald Reagan's daughter, Maureen, and her husband, Dennis Revell, both saw Lincoln's transparent form next to the bedroom's fireplace. Kennedy's Press Secretary James Haggerty admitted to sensing the presence of Lincoln's ghost in the White House, and Clinton's Press Secretary Mike McCurry admitted he was a believer: 'There are, from time to time, reports that the White House is haunted by mysterious appearances of figures from history, and I believe them. There have been serious people who have serious tales to tell about these encounters, and there are many people who seriously believe that there is a haunting quality to the White House.'"

Hillary Clinton—who famously "channeled" the spirit of Eleanor Roosevelt—mentioned a spooky feeling, as did Jenna Bush, who claimed she heard Twenties music coming from a fireplace in the bedroom she occupied, though, of course, no such music was playing.

It seems undeniable that certain buildings and locales have spiritual forces attached to them, as do certain people. "I will also remove the prophets and the unclean spirit from the land," says the passage from *Zechariah—indicating* that indeed occult activities leave an attachment to an area.

In Bernards Township, New Jersey, is a spot called the "Devil's Tree" that was once said to have been the old head-quarters for the Ku Klux Klan and where now an unnatural warmth is felt (preventing snow from accumulating, or so it is reported, during *winter*). This also has been reported near a castle in Western New York and here we need the *Prayer to the Archangel Michael* (for at times ghostly episodes may be demons).

On the other hand, the opposite may occur: a revenant may seem like an evil spirit because a nasty person makes for a nasty spirit. They seem to garner energy by instilling fear, or by creating tension. Many are those who feel different emotions in various rooms in their homes, or even different spots in the same room, indicating the presence of a spirit or its "memory." We don't know how this works. Is the spirit there—or is it a residual effect? Might it be projecting thoughts there from elsewhere? Arguments may erupt out of nowhere. Or there may be a baffling loss of energy—a feeling of exhaustion that should be eradicated through Mass and prayer (particularly the Rosary), for a spirit can infest in such a way as to cause illness. "Cleaning house" is thus an important chore in spiritual health. No spirit of the deceased—"good" or "evil"—should be allowed to linger. Though unintended, their effects can be negative.

"Spirits will remain earthbound because they are attached to a place or a thing," claims a woman from Ohio who specializes in helping spiritually-plagued families. "I always think of these ghosts as being the people who never quite believed the famous phrase, 'you can't take it with you.'" She says she has noted such problems when children won't stay in a room, pets react strangely, or there is sudden tension or illness in a particular location. "Other folks may have built a house and raised a family there," she adds. "And now their spirits don't want to leave. Perhaps someone else cannot bear the thought of a life without their beloved sports car or her treasured piece of jewelry. Or maybe it's just that they don't want anyone else to get their hands on these things. Some of the most commonly 'cursed' places are hotels or bed-and-breakfasts and resorts."

So common are eerie feelings at theatres that often there is a "ghost light" left on for them twenty-four hours a day. Is this wise or does it entice them? The Comedy Store on Sunset Boulevard in Los Angeles is notoriously haunted— with chairs that pile up on each other in an aisle moments after being neatly stacked and candles that relight them- selves—while a restaurant in West Hollywood is said to be haunted by the ghost of a famous rock singer who used the building (and specifically the spot where there is now a bathroom) to record in. The building "moans." Lights pop on and off. The bathroom door handle jiggles by itself. That can occur when a deceased person is overly memorialized, or again with occult, drug, sexual, or criminal practices. Many are those who carry a darkness or "dirtiness" around them, like "baggage." Jesus Himself used the word "ghost"

(*Luke* 24:39) as well as "unclean spirits" (*Zechariah* 13:2, *Matthew* 10:1, *Matthew* 12:43, *Mark* 1:23, *Mark* 1:26, and so forth). The question is whether unclean is always demonic or, as stated, may be a soul in need of purgation.

"Those at a higher level of purgatory are identifiable, while those at lower levels are dark," says Father Mark Bozada, a priest in St. Louis who has been "seeing" spirits since he was a young boy (and carries the Eucharist with him in public places, especially airports, because of them). "I can see the faces of the ones closer to the upper levels of purgatory. Sometimes they do get stuck. I did a house blessing in Kansas City where the home had a presence of children. It turned out that it was part of the 'trail of tears'— deceased Indian children who had been in tribes that had passed through Missouri and had gone to reservations. These spirits are found where you have higher concentrations of people and they do follow people, especially if they think they will be prayed for. The poor souls come like beggars. Mainly it's an interior 'seeing' like the series of mirrors in a reflector telescope. The exterior visions are a confirmation. If there's a place that's infested, I would know the difference between a ghost and a demon. Devils come raging and are often attached to intense evil activity." Praying for the soul of a family member, he says, can often free a home from misfortunes, addictions, or ailments that can be carried by a spirit down a family line. When the soul enters its proper place in the afterlife, he says, the affliction lifts.

Again we see it rooted in the Bible. Says *Matthew*: "Jesus summoned His twelve disciples and gave them authority over unclean spirits, to cast them out, and to heal every kind of disease and every kind of sickness"—indicating that such spirits can cause sickness.

"Throwing him into convulsions, the unclean spirit cried out with a loud voice and came out of him," says *Mark* 1:26—hinting at something like epilepsy.

"When He got out of the boat," *Mark* says further on, "immediately a man from the tombs with an unclean spirit met Him"—now hinting, as I mentioned, that such spirits may linger near burial areas.

"When Jesus saw that a crowd was rapidly gathering, He rebuked the unclean spirit, saying to it, 'You deaf and mute spirit, I command you, come out of him and do not enter him again'" showing the spirits can cause specific ailments, and should be named.

In the view of Father Bozada, "a demon that is present makes you feel like you're falling into a dark hole—cold and menacing with intense fear," as opposed to the uncanny feeling from a revenant.

Chapter 6

Negative spirits play the extremes. They cause mood swings, or lead us to obsession. Sometimes, they may pass on their gluttony or perversion. It is when our spirits are out of balance (and away from Christ) that we are most susceptible. They can gain entrance. Positive ones, on the other hand, are simply looking for prayers or come to comfort us.

Because it's difficult to know which is which, we stay away from direct contact, except to pray for their disposition.

"Probably the largest group of souls remaining in the world of ghosts after death are all those who during their lives were so attached to worldly matters that they're incapable of freeing themselves from them," notes a Polish psychotherapist named Wanda Pratinicka who specializes in deliverance. "These matters can be material or non-material. It can be a house, a car, or other possessions. Everyone has surely heard of haunted houses and the ghosts that terrorize them. Others loved to eat, drink, take drugs, indulge in sex, or gamble to excess. Others again were too fond of making decisions for their near and dear ones, butting into everything, so now they find it too hard to surrender their authority. Another reason for ghosts to remain is a desire to put right the errors they made. They think that by staying on this side they will have an opportunity to mend what they did badly. There are also ghosts who cannot leave in peace because a curse has been put on them, black arts have been used against them. Another sizable group is comprised of those who committed suicide. Some souls find it hard to leave earth because they've left someone who, in their opinion, should be looked after. These might be a parent of a small child, or a solicitous child with elderly and lonely parents, and so on. The souls remain on earth because that is the decision they took."

When they infiltrate a living person they can cause effects often masked as psychological problems, as they can also transmit illness, or at least symptoms. The psychotherapist claims that tumors have left "cancer" patients when "ghosts" who had suffered tumors were themselves cast out.

These are controversial notions that are hard to discern. When there are signs, it could mean a soul has been allowed by God to send an omen. Still, we should not act as if the dead belong among the living. This can cause them to hang around (in a way that is not beneficial). But there are times when their visits seem positive.

When they come to comfort?

"I lost my beloved son at the age of 42 on November 15, 2007," said Rosemary Russo of White Plains, New York. "He left a wife and eight-year-old daughter. The July before he died, his daughter, and my son's wife, and I went to see the July Fourth fireworks at a local park. He was feeling very ill that night and we left before the fireworks because he was too weak to remain. The July after he died, his wife, daughter, and I went back to that park for the July Fourth fireworks and we stayed to see them. He had been very upset that his daughter missed them because of his illness.

We all felt a strong sense of his presence. That night I took my granddaughter home to sleep over. She had fallen asleep in my bed and I was sitting on the edge of the bed when I heard a *whooshing* sound and turned around and I saw a white figure, cloudlike, rising above her.

"I could see the head and arms, which were outstretched, and the rest of the figure was cloudlike and bright but not outlined. It was like a mist. I recognized his profile. Unmistakably I knew that it was my son. His head was turned to one side. The whole corner of the ceiling was bright white around him. I felt a sense of calm. It dissipated and I lay down and went to sleep. I was not asleep. I didn't dream it. I know that was him."

For most, it is the *sense* of a person.

"When we were able to visit our dwelling for a twenty-four hour period after the destruction of Hurricane Katrina, I approached my house where there was devastation to my patio covering and the roof of my home, along with a broken window that had been totally torn away by debris," Valerie Powers of Marrero, Louisiana, told me. "When my nephew and I were trying to patch up the broken window so no further rain-wind could damage the interior of my house, the presence of my mother Rose, who had passed away just three years earlier, was *surrounding* us. I could actually feel her with us, standing right behind us to observe and help. It moved me so much that I just literally could not stop crying."

And then there are the dreams that are more than dreams.

They are indelible.

When Rose Laumbach Monreal's 18-year-old son Steven died in a car accident, her consolation came through what she calls two "visitation dreams." "A visitation dream from a loved one is a dream in which you can actually touch them, talk to them, smell them, and observe what they are wearing," she says. "The loved one is actually visiting through the dream. It is a true, real visitation. You awake from a visitation dream knowing with all your soul that you were with your loved one." In the first, on June 30, 2003, Steven came to her as a child. "We were sitting in the living room as if waiting for someone to arrive," writes the Austin, Texas, woman in a touching book. "I remember my mom, dad, my sister Liz, my nephew Jimmy, and my brother Michael being in the room. He first went to my sister Liz and she hugged him and told him hello. Then he progressed around the room, telling everyone hello and giving them a hug. He was close to my brother Michael. As he approached him, he handed him a wrapped gift." When the boy got to Rose, he said, "Mom, I love you soooooo much!" She said, "Steven, I love you forever and ever!" Cryptically, her son responded, "Mom, guess what? I have two new best friends." He said their names but Rose does not recall them. She asked when she could be with him, "for I didn't want to be here without him." He replied, "Mom, I live far, far away now. You will see me again one day, I promise. I have to go now." Rose woke elated, and had a second "visitation dream" in June of 2008. In that second one, intriguingly enough, Rose encountered Steven after praying to the Virgin of Guadalupe to see him again. The dream began with her sitting on a bench near what was kind of like an old waiting station or train depot. "I looked around at the surroundings," she says. "There wasn't any type of vegetation. It seemed almost to be another planet. There was no noise, only silence. As I looked to the horizon, I saw a figure appear. As it got closer, I realized it was Steven. He came running. We embraced. He had the biggest smile on his face. He looked radiant. As he approached me, I reached out and realized I could actually touch him. I remember we hugged and kissed each other. It seemed to go on and on. We laughed and just were so happy to see each other. I touched his hair. I remember his smell." When she asked if he was alive or dead, the boy replied, "Mom, I am neither alive nor dead. Maria makes me this way so we can come and visit you." In fact, he was so happy, she recalls, "It's as if he glowed." He was wearing clothes she had never seen before. So many mysteries!

A woman named Lulie Cosby whose daughter Christin died on Palm Sunday 1998 in another accident heard from a friend whose daughter-in-law had a football-sized tumor in her colon. "One evening around sunset, she was walking atop one of the many beautiful mountains in the area," noted Christin's mother. "The sun rays were shining beautifully through the trees and she was praying fervently to God to please help her daughter-in-law recover. She said that all of a sudden, she felt very peaceful and knew without a doubt that everything would be alright. At that time, she saw a little fawn to her right. She looked at it and it ran across her path to her left. As she followed it with her eyes, she saw Christin. The fawn ran behind her. Christin smiled and communicated to her the following: *'Everything will be alright and tell everyone that I am alright.'* After that, Christin was gone. My friend fell to her knees crying. The next morning, she went to the hospital to check on her daughter-in-law and found out that the tumor was not malignant and she would be released from the hospital soon."

Usually, the communication comes in a way that is just short of proof. Always, there is room left for faith. Sometimes it involves what seem like unexplained sounds. "My uncle died a tragic death, in essence drinking and smoking himself to death at an early age," wrote Mike Birkhold of Kalamazoo Michigan. "On the night of his funeral, I was lying in bed, not yet asleep. Suddenly, I heard steps crossing my bedroom in front of the bed. I was initially frightened but then I had a strong sense that this was my uncle and he wanted me to pray for his soul. I immediately began praying for Uncle Mac and the footsteps stopped. I then felt at peace and fell asleep."

Often involving nature, the signs can be beautiful ones.

"When my wife was diagnosed with stage-four breast cancer on October 20, my brother handed me a first-class relic of St. Paul of the Cross," recalled Matt from Shawnee, Kansas. "I didn't know at the time that October 20th is his feast day. My wife and I met on July 7, sixteen years to the day I said goodbye to her. At her grave, a bluebird landed on the tree above. This was significant because she loved blue-birds and went to a place called 'Camp Bluebird' for cancer patients. I asked out loud, 'Nanci, did you send that?' And suddenly a gust of wind blew the wing off of a plastic butterfly my children had placed there days earlier . . ."

Pam Eichen of central Minnesota had gone to the grave of a deceased grandchild to pray for her father-in-law—who was in a fatal coma. "As I stood there, I asked my grandson to tell Grandpa it was okay to go up to Heaven because poor Grandma couldn't go on much longer," Pam recounted. "All of a sudden, I felt a tremendous sense of peace and joy. I looked at my watch and it was 7:10 p.m. As I slowly drove back to the hospital, I experienced the most wonderful sensation of pure joy and I knew my father-in-law was with God. When I walked back to my father-in-law's hospital room, his minister had just arrived and all of the family were joining hands in prayer. I asked them what time he died, and they told me it was 7:10 p.m."

Major disasters bring out the accounts.

There was 9/11.

On the morning of the attacks, one woman named Bonnie McEneaney—still holding out hope—went outside and yelled to her husband, "Eamon where are you?" Suddenly the trees rustled. Their branches swayed. As a little river of wind swirled around her, she knew he was gone. The couple had shared a joke about quarters and after his death quarters began appearing everywhere. "I would get up out of bed in the middle of the night to check on my kids and I'd come back to bed and there'd be a quarter in my bed," she said.

After 9/11, another widow, Monica Iken, woke up only to see her husband Michael standing at the foot of the bed. "He was glowing, and I just sat up," she told ABC News. "I said, 'Thank you for coming.' As quick as I said that, he left. But he was smiling. He was telling me he was there with me. He was literally standing there."

More often, it is subtle.

From Peg Christopher in the Charlotte, North Carolina area: "On May 5, in 1983, I was on a plane (Eastern Airlines Flight 855) that lost all three engines and fell approximately 13,000 to 16,000 feet. After the pilot said, 'Ditching is imminent,' and we were in crash position, I visually and spiritually perceived the presence of my mother as she moved onto the plane from the window and passed in front of me— settling next to me on the left, near the aisle. *I felt a tremendous sense of peace* and the overwhelming fear left me. My mother had died in 1979."

This is another place where those who have spiritual gifts say they encounter spirits—airplanes.

Is it simply because a lot of people are in a small area or because revenants draw from the nervous energy?

Or that they have an "attachment"?

There was a famous bestseller that recounted the bizarre details of strange happenings that came in the aftermath of an airline crash. The strange tales of ghostly airmen even appeared in a 1974 edition of the U.S. Flight Safety Foundation's newsletter—so widely circulated were the accounts in this normally strait-laced (if not quite down-to-earth) industry. "Perhaps the most extraordinary and credible research into the ghost phenomenon ever documented is the so-called 'Ghosts of Flight 401,'" says a near-death website.

"On December 29 of 1972, an Eastern Airlines Tri-Star jetliner, Flight 401, crashed into a Florida swamp. The pilot, Bob Loft, and flight engineer, Don Repo, were two of the 101 people who perished in the air crash. Not long after the crash, the ghosts of Loft and Repo were seen on more than twenty occasions by crew members on other Eastern Tri-Stars, especially those planes which had been fitted with parts salvaged from the Flight 401 wreckage. The apparitions of Loft and Repo were invariably described as being extremely lifelike. They were not only reported by people who had known Loft and Repo, but their ghosts were also subsequently identified from photographs by people who had not known Loft and Repo."

A flight attendant named Beverly Raposa once wrote to recall how she survived that crash when, there in the Florida Everglades, the escape chute and wreckage seemed miraculously to form a shield around her. It reminded her of a statue she carried of the Blessed Mother, which she had purchased in the chapel at JFK International Airport in New York.

The statue depicted Mary perched on a propeller, with a jet on her mantle and one side of her veil extended.

Chapter 7

There are saints. There are angels. There are the deceased.

For all we know, we are watched over by ancestors of whom we have no knowledge—but will meet one day when we die and see our entire lineage.

Mystics inform us that there are more spirits at a Mass—angels and saints—than living humans (and that we would practice far more reverence if we could see into that invisible world).

But let us recognize the negative aspect.

Spirits that do not move on to the other side can affect us.

When a psychiatrist named Dr. George Ritchie "died" during an illness, he claimed to have been shown this spiritual dynamic by Jesus, Who allegedly took him on a tour of the invisible reality around us.

In a book called *Return from Tomorrow*, Dr. Ritchie wrote of visiting various places and in one case was inside "humming factories and office buildings—where I could see easily as I could see the streets—too many people at the machines and desks. In one room a gray-haired man was sitting in an armchair dictating a letter into a rotating cylinder. Standing behind him, not an inch away, another man, maybe ten years older, kept snatching repeatedly at the speaking tube as though he would tear it from the seated man's hand. 'No!' he was saying, 'if you order a hundred gross at a time they'll charge more. Take a thousand gross at a time. Pierce would have given you a better deal. Why did you send Bill on that Treadwell job?' On and on he went, correcting, giving orders, while the man in the chair appeared neither to see nor hear him. I noticed the phenomenon repeatedly, people unaware of others right beside them. I saw a group of assembly-line workers gathered around a coffee canteen. One of the women asked another for a cigarette, begged her in fact, as though she wanted it more than anything in the world. But the other one, chatting with her friends, ignored her. She took a pack of cigarettes from her coveralls, and without ever offering it to the woman who reached for it so eagerly, took one out and lit it. Fast as a striking snake the woman who had been refused snatched at the lighted cigarette in the other one's mouth. With a chill of recognition I saw that she was unable to grip it."

Was the spirit in the office just trying to help—or a soul who was still too attached to his business?

In the case of the cigarette, it was addiction—as was also true in a further stunning case in which Dr. Ritchie— whose accounts spurred the modern research into near-death experiences—was drawn "inside a dingy bar and grill near what looked like a large naval base.

"A crowd of people, many of them sailors, lined the bar three deep, while others jammed wooden booths along the wall," he once wrote. "Though a few were drinking beer, most of them seemed to be belting whiskies as fast as the two perspiring bartenders could pour them. Then I noticed a striking thing. A number of the men standing at the bar seemed unable to lift their drinks to their lips. Over and over

I watched them clutch at their shot glasses, hands passing through the solid tumblers, through the heavy wooden counter top, through the very arms and bodies of the drinkers around them. And these men, every one of them, lacked the aureole of light that surrounded the others. And it was obvious that these living people, the light-surrounded ones, the ones actually drinking, talking, jostling each other, could neither see the desperately thirsty disembodied beings among them, nor feel their frantic pushing to get at those glasses. (Though it was clear to me, watching, that the non-solid people could both see and hear each other. Furious quarrels were constantly breaking out among them over glasses that none could actually get to their lips). I watched one young sailor rise unsteadily from a stool, take two or three steps, and sag heavily to the floor. I was staring in amazement as the bright cocoon around the unconscious sailor simply opened up. It parted at the very crown of his head and began peeling away from his head, his shoulders. Instantly, quicker than I'd ever seen anyone move, one of the insubstantial beings who had been standing near him at the bar was on top of him. He had been hovering like a thirsty shadow at the sailor's side, greedily following every swallow the young man made. Now he seemed to spring at him like a beast of prey. In the next instant, the springing figure had vanished. Twice more, as I stared, stupefied, the identical scene was repeated. A man passed out, a crack swiftly opened in the aureole round him, one of the non-solid people vanished as he hurled himself at the opening, almost as if he had scrambled inside the other man."

We see then how our behavior can attract spirits—the wrong kind—and even cause an infestation. I have seen the case where a daughter takes on the personality of the mother, and is nearly incommunicado.

The opposite occurs with the presence of angels. They are light and airy. And they too are a constant influence. As

Dr. Jeffrey Long recounts, a man named Jonathan had a one percent chance of surviving surgery on his esophagus. But he did, and later told of leaving his body. "I remember standing about ten feet up and ten feet to the side of my body on the operating table," Jonathan recounted to Dr. Long. "Around the table were at least a dozen nurses and doctors. But what was so emotional was the presence of glowing people who I can only describe as angels. Each angel was guiding the hands of the staff they were standing next to. I don't remember details too specific, such as what tools were used or the exact position of my body, but only because I was focused so much on the angels guiding the staff in everything they did, from walking to the use of the tools within my chest cavity. Even after the operation, I still had an unusual peace and no fear. The doctor said it was the best operation he had ever gone through—there were no problems at all—and he was impressed at my rate of recovery."

We thus see that our lives are often and even usually affected by hidden orchestration. It's praying for the angels that gets us to the place of safety. If there's a disturbance in a house, or something is sensed, it's wise to begin praying for the soul to head for the Light of Jesus (in the event it is earthbound) and also to cast out any possible evil being in the Name of Jesus (in case it's a demon). It's also efficacious to ask the Blessed Mother to "clean" your home (she is "immaculate"). Ask the Archangel Michael to come. Invoke the hierarchy. Some angels are bigger. Some brighter. They can be large and translucent and shielding and comforting. Their light is so intense that it makes you think everything is okay. "Their faces were brilliant and their long blonde to brown silky hair blended with their feathers and long flowing robes," said one who had a deathbed glimpse. They may come as a flash. They may come as mysterious strangers. For some reason, it seems like corners of rooms are where they enter (along with other spirits). "After the light disseminated, there were about twenty spheres, which transformed into her father, her mother, and many other beings she called angels," writes Dr. John Lerma of another dying patient's experience. "She described her parents as being human in appearance and around their late twenties to early thirties. The angels were of varying colors and sizes, and different personalities. Two or three angels were the most beautiful color of Aegean blue and about seven-feet tall with a jovial, witty attitude. They were making her laugh by tickling her soul with their feathers. Their eyes were iridescent, the 'blue' to 'green' colors I've never seen. They pierced my very soul and filled me with God's love and peace. Whatever they looked at took on God's love and peace, and it gleamed with joy."

Angels can appear any way they want. Sometimes, as was mentioned, there are the feathers—and cases in which actual feathers have been left behind (as a "sign"). They can be seen "flying" and frolicking around a room. They can tower or be as short as four feet. They seem to float or hover in midair and can arrive like small comets or leave with an immensely bright luminosity. During spiritual warfare, they may appear with flowing deep maroon or blazing white robes. In one case a bright light near a dying man's bed seemed to come from one part of the room and a smoke-like entity came from another corner. The darkness slowly moved toward the patient, causing seizures. This has been frequently reported by nurses.

Fill your home with angels, leaving no space for anything untoward. Use Holy Water. Although we are not to fear (which can feed them power, as can overly discussing them), there are dangers. Recall *Ephesians* 6 to "put on the full armor of God, so that you will be able to stand firm against the schemes of the devil. For our struggle is not against flesh and blood, but against the rulers, against the powers, against the world forces of this darkness, against the spiritual forces of wickedness in the heavenly places." Dark forces surround us just as the bright ones do. They are deceptive. Scripture tells us that they can even come as "an angel of light." They may masquerade as a deceased acquaintance, and, too, if a revenant, we must also realize that the spirit of a deceased person will have the same personality as the person—until that spirit has been purified by going into Christ's Light.

A strange drain in energy—fatigue—can be a sign that a spirit is drawing from you and we don't want that. We also look for anxiety, confusion, and contention as first signs that what's around is negative. Sudden withdrawal, bad habits, unexplained changes of mind, drinking, hoarding, compulsive eating, sloth, ill temper, and foul language can be indicators. Certain cases of autism have been cured through deliverance, as have allergies. "The 'hidden' evil spirits at large in the world can manifest themselves by God's permissive Will—if not by their actual appearance, at least by their power—as happened twice in the case of *Job* (1:12 and 2:6)," writes an expert, Father John Hampsch of California, who cites some of the same biblical passages I previously mentioned. "The Old Testament indicates that God's chosen people, the Israelites, had no difficulty in believing in the manifestation of deceased persons as living, even though the word 'ghost' wasn't part of their daily vocabulary. This belief is clear from the story about Maccabeus's otherworld visitors, Onias and Jeremiah (*2 Maccabees* 15:12-16); and Samuel's ghostly posthumous admonishment of Saul from the abode of the dead (*1 Samuel* 28). And in *Sirach* 46:20 Samuel prophesies from the grave. Other direct or indirect biblical allusions to 'ghosts': *Job* 4:15: 'A spirit glided by my face and the hair on my body stood on end.' This 'spirit' may have been an angel; but it does give us a hint of even a tactile human experience of meeting a spiritual entity. *Leviticus* 19:31 tells us that there are dangerous spirits to be eschewed. From the insights and wisdom of doctors of the Church like St. Thomas Aquinas, as well as modern spiritual writers, plus the anecdotal testimony from credible people, the existence and activity of the spirit world is fairly well known. That it is possible for spirits to communicate in dreams and in wakeful states and to experience a possible bodily reaction to the visitation, see *Job* 4:15.

"In the spirit world are many evil entities, unseen but only occasionally manifested," continues the esteemed priest. "Only when certain very restricted conditions are fulfilled can these entities become externally manifest.

"Some of these disconcerting spirit-entities are 'poltergeists' and others are 'ghosts.' Poltergeists are not humans but devilishly mischievous evil spirits; they're mostly rather stupid, and in the hierarchy of the nefarious, they're the underlings of the underworld. However, they sometimes seem to act in partnership with deceased human persons— often persons who have died recently in a state of bitterness, hatred, or unforgiveness of their enemies (especially refusing to forgive hurtful relatives or associates). Spirits may act *through* or *with* disembodied human souls who formerly lived in the locale where the poltergeist event occurs—near cemeteries, above curse-infected burial spots, in their former homes that have become 'haunted' houses or victims of evil actions like murder, torture, abortion, incest, pedophilia, or where occultic practices occurred—by psychics, palm readers, fortune-tellers, and especially places of Satanic covens. The name poltergeist comes from the German word *poltern*, which means to knock, and *geist*, which means spirit. Typically they disturb by knocking or noise-making, but also by more pernicious acts of object-moving, stone-throwing, fire-igniting, etcetera. They are more difficult to expel than ghosts."

I may disagree with Father Hampsch on certain things (I'm not sure a poltergeist is necessarily so dumb, nor that it is always a demon, for a deceased human can also be loud and mischievous; some argue that most negative entities are revenants), but there's no doubt spirits infest people and rooms and homes and entire communities. In Florida near Orlando on Interstate Four (I-4) at the St. John's River is a stretch where police say there is a mysterious frequency of serious car crashes and reports that this highway was built over an old grave. Some report spotting "smoke" or even apparitions. A television station in Orlando says the road where most crashes occur cradles the graves of a family of four dating back to the 1880s and a place once called St. Joseph Catholic Colony. Known as the "I-4 Dead Zone," one newspaper described it as a "small stretch" where "hundreds of people have been killed or injured in crashes." Since 1963, said the station, 2,000 accidents have been reported there—a phenomenal number. It is also near a swath of trees bent over when the eyes of three hurricanes passed over the region in 2004, and is also in the path on occasion of tornadoes (as is an eerie part of Xenia, Ohio). I myself have seen incredible displays of lightning in this vicinity. Notes a website: "As soon as the building began over the graves, things started to happen. Hurricane Donna, known as one of the worst hurricanes in Central Florida, eerily made its way right over the site of the graves with the eye of the hurricane sitting above the new construction site of I-4. This could just be a coincidence, but what was weird was how the hurricane got there. It started out breaking land from the Atlantic Ocean in South Florida. It then moved across the state completely to the Gulf of Mexico, but then it moved back onto land and started moving up the newly made I-4. Hurricane Donna's eye lay over the graves at around midnight after its second landfall. It was several months before construction of I-4 could continue due to the extreme damage of Hurricane Donna, which made people think it was the dead fighting back from their resting place. Ever since the highway was completed, people have reported seeing ghosts along the highway, ghost hitchhikers in their cars, phantom trucks, and orbs crossing the highway. Some people say that when they are on their cell phones in this spot that weird unrecognizable voices will come on the line interrupting their conversations. Radio stations have been known to go from a perfectly clear signal to static and sometimes even eerie voices will be heard over the radio speaker. Some of those who lived through their accident claimed they swerved to not hit the family of four crossing the street. Others say they hit a few people. However no people or bodies were ever found."

Chapter 8

Is it all due to a small grave? Perhaps. Prayers need to be said, for sure. Is there something more? Consider that the area is also known for old Indian burial graves, and old Indian sites are notorious for drawing "spirits." We find this across America. The I-4 zone is next to Lake Monroe and in a secluded area nearby is an old Seminole burial mound.

So prevalent were Seminoles that the county's named for them.

About ten miles from there is Cassadaga—a hamlet inhabited by mediums, psychics, and fortune-tellers known as "spiritualists." Séances are constantly held, and each Halloween, visitors can sit on the devil's chair (or "Seat of Satan")—a bench near a cemetery where any request to the devil is (supposedly) answered.

It is interesting that Cassadaga was founded by spiritualists who have a similar village in Western New York that's also Indian territory and also known for strong thunderstorms. Legend has it the mediums at this place, which is called Lily Dale, were directed by an Indian spirit to start Cassadaga as a winter haven.

Just to the west of Cassadaga are Orlando and its famous attractions, now including a theme park dedicated to Harry Potter.

We thus see how things weave in and out—and how spiritual energies attract, enhance, and accumulate. Other mounds can be found near Savannah, Georgia, which has a history of piracy and voodoo and is reckoned by many to be the most "haunted" city in the U.S. (if not Savannah, then New Orleans, which also is known for voodoo and which was struck, of course, by that great hurricane called "Katrina," which means "purification"). The voodoo was imported from Haiti, which is also disaster-prone.

Is that merely a coincidence? Fate? A curse?

On a thirty-five-mile stretch of road south of Harare in Zimbabwe, Africa, are incredible crashes. One killed the prime minister's wife. Days later, there was another that injured fifteen more common folk and was attributed to angry ancestors (as in most of Africa, there is strong belief in veneration of the dead). On the same road—a few miles closer to Harare—eleven traders were killed when a bus crashed through concrete and after Christmas that same year twelve members of a family died when a bus hit their truck. "When they're passing that area, some drivers see people with their eyes when there's nobody on the road," claimed a local chief to a newspaper.

We see it with entire cities and countries but especially with families. In England a twin brother died in a crash at the same spot where his brother had succumbed in similar fashion.

What was following them?

Meanwhile, in Maryland, a school principal from Silver Spring was slain inside his home, which had been the scene of two previous murders (and had been exorcised by ministers precisely for that reason).

Almost fifteen years after saving his future wife's life at a gas station (from an attack by her then-husband), a Michigan police officer died—of a heart attack—at the same station.

Another hospital account:

"I was sitting in the dining room with the lights off, charting by the dimmed hall lights, when I caught something out of the corner of my eye moving down the hall," relates a nurse. "Thinking it was one of my 'wanderers,' I looked up and saw what to this day I still believe was a toddler on a tricycle. Let me tell you now, I lost it. The admittance book went flying and I skittered up the short hallway to the nurse's station. I relayed my story to the charge nurse and she just sort of chuckled at my expression and explained that one of the residents who had passed away years ago had a grandson who had been killed by the back tires of her car. He was in the driveway and she didn't see him and backed right over him. The night the lady died, she was calling out, 'Tyler, oh my baby, Tyler. Nana's coming.'"

Are we to chalk it up as happenstance when tragedy plagues an area or a family? Is it coincidence that cultures from Buddhist to Catholic have cleansing prayers? Do some locales have a supernatural "memory"?

At old battlefields are often claims of hearing gunshots or glimpsing ghostly apparitions of soldiers from past centuries. Go to Fort Niagara in Western New York and the guides will recount their experiences.

Chapter 9

Among the most haunted places in the U.S.: dungeons and covens, along with battlefields. Spirits attach to past deeds, and may even cause tragedies or scenes to replay. At certain spots mysterious hitchhikers may be reported (in some cases, they seem to be angels). People are also haunted. Darkness draws the wrong kind of spirits. When around, these spirits may be activated or enhanced by the spiritual forces of locales we traverse—at times reaching a "critical mass" that can portend an unfortunate event (or series of them).

Sometimes spirits leave their imprint. In flames or wreckage, eerie faces are seen (on occasion).

Anything occult can also lead to peculiar happenings. In England a "pagan psychic" died in what the coroner called "an unusual combination of events" when he had a heart attack, veered up a bank, and the car's catalytic converter set the grass ablaze (burning him alive).

Meanwhile, unusually potent tornadoes often target the single town of Xenia, Ohio—which the Indians knew as the "place of the devil wind." Meteorologists call it inexplicable.

More than anything, our sins (especially the seven deadly ones) cause energies to swirl around us, as do emotions. Ghosts, some believe, look for energy. It is something that everyone can feel when they are near it, or when they come into permanent contact with an environment that's full of hatred and dark oppressive power. This bad energy can bring sicknesses and accidents. In speaking of poltergeists, Father Hampsch notes that "angry spirits may partner with dead humans but are often attracted by *living* humans (good and bad) as transmitters ('magnet' persons) to download their paranormal energy, although other 'non-transmitting' humans who are present can see and hear the sometimes frightening phenomena. Usually, for some unknown reason, but not always, the 'magnet' or person who attracts poltergeists is young, frequently in his or her adolescence or puberty. Girls seem to attract poltergeists somewhat more often than boys. The poltergeist-attracting person is often under emotional stress or insecure and emotionally dysfunctional, or has been psycho-traumatized by incest, rape, injury, rejection, and frightening events of the past. Young who have had abortions or people on drugs, or who are gang members, or fornicators, are the *strongest* attracters of poltergeists. However, emotionally and spiritually-balanced persons can also attract poltergeists, but far less frequently; in fact, many saints were assailed by poltergeists, such as St. Jerome and John Vianney."

A woman who sees into the spiritual dimensions says that poltergeists are "sly creatures and they creep in wherever they are given an opportunity, and they can cause enormous destruction." Adolph Hitler was plagued at night by a dark shadow that often caused him to call out for his guards. Did a spirit take him over, and did they plague all of Germany (with its history of war "gods"). While such spirits may attack a person who is holy (in demonic retaliation), and while, in other cases, sin draws the curse, it also seems that spirits draw from those who are hyper, angry, or otherwise exude negative energy. Some hypothesize that spirits are associated with lightning because when there is electricity in the atmosphere they can draw from it and materialize. Others point out the abundant nervous energy available at a dentist's office (or, again, a hospital). This is at best speculation, and we need not delve too deeply into the "mechanics." But it's informative to note that spirits can play havoc with electronics, and can also start fires. With prayer, we halt that. With the Rosary, we begin to clear our homes (and family lines) from revenants. For curses can carry through the ages—turning an innocent person into a magnet.

"Now when the unclean spirit goes out of a man, it passes through waterless places seeking rest, and does not find it," says *Matthew* 12:43, which tells us, in essence, that when an unclean spirit leaves one person, it searches over a desert for another place or person to attach. That person may be the relative of a person who has died and had an unclean spirit that's now free and roaming. It's a complex subject that starts right back in the Old Testament where again we see in the account of Maccabeus the reference to otherworldly visitors. (See too *1 Samuel* 28, where the ghost of Samuel admonishes Saul).

And so we see the dynamic around us. There are "vortices." There are places—and people—with strangeness. There is good charisma. There is bad. Some rock stars say that while composing songs they felt like they were "channeling" from a spirit—and we see the frenzy in crowds of young people that result. To cleanse, we should fast. John Lennon said the name "Beatles" was given to him in a dream by a man surrounded by a ring of flames. Was this a purgatorial soul, a demonic spirit, or simply an attempt to describe radiance? Whatever the case, music goes right to the soul and can have profound spiritual repercussions.

There may also be "ghosts" who don't realize that they are ghosts, says Father Hampsch. When they do, they may try to overcome a person. They are confused—caught in the emptiness (desert) of the lives they led. "Although meeting a spirit may be scary, a Godly apparition will lead to peace," says the priest. "A Godly spirit will *always* and without hesitation affirm the Lordship of Jesus Christ. Thus we need to test the spirit with the formula of *1 John* 4:1-3." The famous mystic Maria Esperanza saw deceased souls around people. Doubtless, so did St. Padre Pio. There are happy ghosts—deceased relatives working for God at consoling or helping those on earth—and also ones that are full of malice. They are deceptive.

While we should not automatically treat an unsettled spirit as evil, neither should we cotton up to such an entity—even when they profess Jesus. Nor should we speak too much about a spirit, lest we energize it. "Usually they are persons who have died while resisting God's Plan for leaving this world when called by death to the next world," writes Father Hampsch. "Some have become ghosts by violently resisting God's design of their death, and others by pre-empting God's design for death by choosing suicide. Some of the 'bewildered souls' show no intent of inflicting harm; these souls are disturbed but not disturbing. But other ghosts are very obnoxious, or even violent, generally perpetuating the behavior patterns they had when alive. Ghosts are fairly easily dispelled by either private or ritual prayers to break any posthumous bondage the deceased person may be under."

Indeed, these issues were tackled by a brilliant Jesuit priest named Father Herbert Thurston, who died in 1939—after meticulously documenting many haunted cases where objects were flung around rooms by poltergeists. His observations were granted special attention because he was considered the epitome of a highly discerning Jesuit scholar—one who didn't believe most claims but became convinced that homes in fact can become plagued by negative forces. After lengthy investigation, Father Thurston concluded that some cases are caused by demons and others by unsettled spirits, meaning that where a Mass for the repose of a soul may clear some situations—along with simple loving commands for the spirit to go to the Light—in other cases there may be the need for deliverance. Relics, holy pictures, medals, and other blessed items often help (especially the Sacred Heart), although at times the issue goes beyond that—necessitating, said Father Thurston, a full-scale exorcism.

When a building is consecrated, he pointed out, the threshold is blessed by the bishop with the mark of the Cross and the proclamation, *Ecce crucis signum, fugiant phantasmata cuncta* ("behold the emblem of the Cross; let all specters flee").

Unfortunately, in our day, few take the prayer literally.

Not just devils but also spirits of the dead often need to be expelled, but this is a matter rarely broached by priests (due to simple lack of training, knowledge, or experience). During the past hundred years, many clergy have been indoctrinated into the tenets of psychology, which all but ignore the supernatural. And so the devil is in the shadows. That includes the shadows of psychology. Cleverly, he had convinced us to think of evil in medical terms. Thus, instead of oppression, or obsession, or possession, we have "neurosis" and "psychosis" and "schizophrenia." We have "multiple personality" when demons are many or "legion." Incredibly, a look at "Anna O," the very female patient whose case made Freud famous, reveals she once protested she was not *mentally* ill but in need of deliverance! Look at the many words used to describe mental states and we see the connotations. Many have a "dark side." The "devil" made them do it. We are "demented." Or "bedeviled." We have our "demons." There are voices (such as those that have led many to homicide, including the man who killed John Lennon).

Satan tempted Eve as a serpent. The Hebrew name for serpent is linked to the word "hiss," one author points out, or "to whisper a magical spell."

Here we see the danger of the occult.

Was *Genesis* the place for the "genesis" of witchcraft (forbidden knowledge, and perhaps forbidden powers)?

Whatever the case may be, hear the "hiss" in psychological terms such as obsession, oppression, depression, and possession (or Hitler's "SS").

Used clinically, these words hide the real workings of the devil or revenant. "Often horror starts to creep in, too," said the Polish deliverance therapist. "The ghosts not only refuse to leave but they also try to frighten the priest more and more. That's why so many priests give it up, and many others watching them don't even start on an exorcism. Many priests are frightened of the devil, his vengeance, and they also fear possessed people. In such cases it is easier to ascribe mental diseases to every symptom and to send the patient off to a hospital just to have at least one case taken off one's hands. But these instances do not diminish; there are more and more of them."

The result is suffering. Our young can be specially targeted. In Africa, schoolgirls are often plagued by alleged entities sent forth by voodooists (creating complete panic), while in India terror was struck in both young and old and an entire community by sightings of an elusive entity they called a "monkey man."

Elsewhere it may be an "abominable snowman," or "mothman," or the "Jersey devil," or an alien. Let us note that St. Columba made the Sign of the Cross and according to legend chased away the Loch Ness "monster." Was it an evil spirit? Was it a deception? During the Middle Ages, bishops exorcised UFOs. "When demons focus on a human habitation or locality, they can cause much suffering and chaos," remarks Father Thomas J. Euteneuer, an exorcist from Virginia. "This is why a third section was added to the exorcism ritual in 1890 which contains the Exorcism of Pope Leo XIII, entitled Exorcism Against Satan and the Fallen Angels, which is an exorcism for places. This same prayer appeared in print officially in the 1925 edition of the *Rituale Romanum*. Demons cannot 'possess' localities because, strictly speaking, they can only possess *living* things. A house can be *infested* with demons that have mysteriously chosen that place or have been invited to that place by some evil or occult practice in its history. It is for that reason that I often advise regular use of Holy Water and blessed salt sprinkled around the entire periphery of a property and throughout communities, along with medals. Sacraments and sacramentals undoubtedly protect us from the power of evil but not because they are magic. They are, rather, spiritual fountains which confer grace, provided that the recipient of these marvelous gifts uses or receives them with faith. The protection of the Church's spiritual resources can be likened to an electrified fence around a house."

Demons, says the priest, often run in packs—dominated by one principle spirit that is the strongest intellect and will of the group.

These entities struggle with us because we are marked for Heaven.

A man named Marino Restrepo who had a near-death-like experience while held captive by kidnappers in his homeland of Colombia says he was shown during that episode how, after fallen angels were thrown out of Heaven, they turned from light into darkness and were separated from the light at the beginning of Creation.

The fallen angels knew that man would occupy the spaces they lost in Heaven," he says; this causes their extreme demonic rage.

"If a saint occupies the place of a fallen angel, then that explains their ferocious battle not to be replaced," Restrepo has written. "The celestial army, by Divine design and through the action of the messenger angels, is in charge of fighting the ongoing battles being waged shoulder to shoulder with the saints here on earth in order to help them achieve celestial glory. The spaces left empty by the fallen angels will be filled by the saints to complete the salvific plan of restoring paradise. St. Paul states in the First Letter to the *Corinthians* (6:3): 'The saints will judge the angels.' I could also see the presence of many other angels—those who were the guardians of my relatives, or people I hurt. I saw the spiritual warfare throughout my life—the struggle between them and the fallen spirits."

We take this to discernment but know that critical in keeping evil forces away is to watch every single thing we think. It is our pride that blinds us. It darkens. To the "hiss" Father Hampsch adds regression (immaturity), repression (avoiding expressions of love), suppression (a bandage over past wounds), and negative thoughts. For a bright future we must let go of the past.

"Repression of love results in repression of joy, peace, and the other segments of the fruit of the Spirit," says Father

Hampsch. "At this point the devil's toehold has become a foothold, and is subtly advancing to become a stronghold."

We must act on the first negative inclination—rooting it out before it sends down its tendrils; for evil grows like a spiny weed and roots deeply and quickly.

One spirit attracts another.

Do they resist?

"The approach of great sinners to his confessional was always heralded by the fierce attacks of baffled spirits," wrote Shane Leslie of John Vianney, the Curé d'Ars, who had many spiritual battles.

Resist they do—but for naught if we are humble.

As stated, we sense demons more than we "encounter" them. Most of their ways are "just below the radar"—so subtle as to not be noticed as a supernatural exchange. The hallmarks are contention, division, and confusion, along with smoldering anger. Evil is goodness reversed; wrong is right and right is wrong (note that the word evil is the word "live" spelled backwards). It is through deep prayer that we cast these things out:

"I command you, spirit of [whatever afflicts you], in the Name of Jesus, to leave my body and home and go to the foot of the Cross to be disposed of according to the Will of God in the Name of Jesus, in the Name of Jesus, in the Name of Jesus, never to return, sealed against. Amen."

Prayers like this can be crucial in clearing what is dark inside of us, be it a demon—which should be forcefully cast away—or a revenant—which we should pray and love toward the Light. *Jesus, Jesus, Jesus.* Remember the power of the Rosary.

Keep clutter out of your home. Physical chaos can attract spirits (at least according to one priest, although chaos is often caused by spirits to begin with). There are many unknown dynamics. An old Christian proverb tells us that "cleanliness is next to Godliness," and this is because one of our best weapons against evil is *discipline*: When we are disciplined, there is less room for entry because we are regulating our thoughts.

Conversion brings miracles.

"My husband Carl was diagnosed with brain cancer in February 2006, became bedridden, and was given a one month survival," a woman named Patricia Heiney of Lake Mead, Pennsylvania, wrote me. "I brought him home. The next five months were the most profound spiritual experience I could ever hope to encounter. He became Catholic in March—a prayer I had for him since the mid-90's at Easter—and I witnessed his transformation of willingly giving up attachments to earthly possessions and a definite quest to forgive and be forgiven for anything. Not one word of complaint from him during this ordeal. It was God's grace that let Carl be with us to July 9, 2006. I believe this was his purgatory on earth and God's gift to me to have him longer. He had three priest-friends for his funeral Mass. Of course, my heart was broken, but at the end of this part of the journey I was deeply somber. The day after he died, I was resting wide awake and my mind was 'talking' to itself and just as if someone interrupted you having a conversation with another, I had the experience.

"I felt a light *squeeze* on my left arm, and saw a vision of his face (with his big happy beautiful eyes and smile), and in a strong voice that I had not heard for months he said, *'Atta girl Patsy.'*

"During his illness I had asked God if at sometime he would let me know Carl was okay and again my prayer was answered. As only a husband and wife would know between them, I understood my husband letting me know that he got to where we prayed he would be one day. I also sensed he was happy with what I could do for him (while he had been with us)."

"When I was in my late twenties, a family friend died at age sixty after a long and lingering illness," added Raven Wenner, whom I have previously quoted. "I stayed a weekend with his brother's family at their farmhouse some weeks after the funeral.

"I always sleep with a rosary, and the first night I was awakened from a sound sleep when I felt someone sit on the left side of my bed and pull me by my right hand into a sitting position.

"Curiously (I only noticed afterward), I kept the rosary in my left hand between me and the person sitting in the moonlight next to me—a handsome man of about thirty, who in a sociable way told me he was very lonely and asked me three times to 'walk with him.'

"Strangely, I was not afraid—only annoyed at the impropriety of a strange gentleman in my bedroom—and the words which came from my mouth three times in reply were, 'Go back where you came from!'

"The gentleman finally rose, looked at me sadly, stepped away from my bed, and disappeared as he backed through the bedroom wall.

Suddenly I realized that it was a dead friend, looking young and healthy if rather lonely and bewildered. I had felt the mattress 'give' as he rose and could still feel the cool touch of his hand on mine. I looked at my watch and it was three am. I stayed awake until dawn to be sure I hadn't dreamed the incident, praying the Rosary for him.

"Next morning over the breakfast table I told my host and his family what had happened and they weren't surprised. They said that their brother/uncle had been visiting as a 'non- scary' ghost since his death six weeks previously. His brother said the first time he came was late at night as the brother was in his office going over farm accounts. The ghost sat down in a chair and said, 'How strange it is to come here without a body!'

"The family was non-practicing Anglican. When I returned home, I went to my parish priest and had a Mass said. Months later (I was working far away by that time) I had a dream of this deceased friend walking away from me down a long dark hall and near the end opening a door in the right-hand wall.

"I couldn't see past the door he opened—but light and birdsong and the perfume of spring flowers poured out the door and illuminated my friend, who turned and gave me a brilliant smile before he entered and closed the door behind him.

"By this I knew—when I awoke—that his time as a ghost had been his purgatory, but now he was safe in Heaven thanks to the Mass offered for him."

Chapter 10

Many are the souls in need of such help and many are they who linger near where they lived or died or are attached to a memory. It is why older cities have ghost tours (which are dangerous). It is why there is a "heaviness" in old places like Europe.

It is also why we must constantly pray for the release of souls.

In Iraq, U.S. marines encountered the paranormal to such an extent at an outpost built on an old grave that a sergeant warned new detachments of strange lights, night-time screams, and the overall eerie atmosphere.

In Uganda, cult members killed in a fire are reported as apparitions on a hillside.

In the former Soviet Union, a strange bonfire was seen hanging in midair, near the ruins of a monastery. This was in the Leningradsky region.

In Georgia on St. Simons Island, ghosts are reported at Dunbar Creek, where in 1803 ten slaves, shackled together and in despair, drowned themselves. (Despite plentiful crabs, fishermen avoid the waterway.)

In Myasnoy Bor near Novgorod, Russia, witnesses have claimed to hear strange sounds in a forest, including songs, laughter, and the clatter of tracks. It is where war dead were found. The language is German.

Are there "anomalous zones"—sort of like time warps—that hold past memories?

After the great Asian tsunami of 2006, many were those who claimed to hear strange sounds and witness apparitions—to the point where it kept tourists away (particularly in Thailand).

These apparitions included a foreign woman whose screams echoed through the night from the wreckage of a hotel that was particularly badly hit, according to BBC. (A security guard on the site left his job because he could not bear it.) There are cries in the night of "help me." In Khao Lak, a local family said their telephone was ringing day and night. When answered, the voices of relatives and friends allegedly cried out "to be rescued from the flames of the crematorium." A taxi driver claimed he picked up six or so tourists one night and felt numb all over and when he peered around, his taxi was empty.

Mostly, hauntings are associated with active spirits. Kings and queens and actresses alike have had their experiences. Stature is irrelevant. Sometimes it is because of the home's history, and in other cases it seems attached to what the person is doing. There are entire books about celebrity ghosts, and celebrities who have seen ghosts. One controversial singer publicly complained that she needed an exorcism; another, Lady Gaga, reportedly feared she was followed by wicked spirits. When director Steven Spielberg was making *Close Encounters of the Third Kind*, there were reports of strange events in hotel rooms used by the crew. The director also made a movie called *Poltergeist*—a movie that seemed cursed by strange events, illnesses, or accidents among those who worked or acted in it (indicating that when we focus on the supernatural without the perspective of Christ, we lack protection). One can also trace unusual tragedies in connection with the show *Bewitched*, movies like *The Exorcist*, *The Omen*, and rock bands that have dabbled with drugs or the occult (or both). After watching a movie called *Paranormal Activity* Spielberg (who has never been associated with drugs or witchcraft, but whose films head in the direction of parapsychology and aliens and spirits) reportedly found himself trapped in his bedroom when his doors locked on their own accord (a locksmith had to be called to get him out). Strange events were associated with a car that famed singer Jimmy Dean purchased and died in.

Years ago, a Christian psychiatrist named Dr. Kenneth McAll from the United Kingdom put together two books filled with cases indicating the problems caused by spirits that won't go on. "Haunting can be such a serious matter and cause severe disturbance for those who have to endure it," he wrote. "My work over the years has led me to recognize the traumatic effects of past family tragedies and evil on the lives of many people living today. In addition to the mental upset caused by tragic or evil events in the family history, I have witnessed many cases in which the upset seemed to stem from the apparent haunting of a place or house in which the affected person had to live. Some people carry their hauntings with them even though they have moved from the house to escape them. When people move to a new house, it is a good idea to have it blessed. I would go further and include prayers for the whole area in a Eucharist as there are many other lost souls still wandering about and needing help and committal to God."

In a book called *Healing the Family Tree*, Dr. McAll recalled: "With eight other people including a priest, I visited Wounded Knee. Here there is a netted enclosure on a small knoll surrounded by rolling hills. It is approached by a gravel track and marks the burial place of the three hundred fifty men, women, and children shot by the American cavalry in 1890. We had decided to hold a service on this spot and, as it was cold, we stayed inside a minivan. As we began the services, a rainstorm blew up which violently rocked the van. The priest interpreted this as an attack by the haunting dead Indian braves. To me, the black clouds seemed to be the Indian women rushing past us in their fury. It all seemed so disturbed that I asked God for a sign that we were doing the right thing. At that moment the clouds opened and a strong ray of sunlight shone through the windscreen right on to the chalice and the wine glowed with a rich red light, then the clouds closed over again and the rain went pouring down. When we ended the service, having confessed to the slaughter and committed the dead to God, the rain stopped, and we were able to go out and walk to the actual burial enclosure with its high heavy netting, an area of ten by twenty feet. We also looked at more recent simple graves, some of them of babies." Dr. McAll claimed that some Indians didn't have burial rites for their dead because "they wanted the resentful dead to continue to haunt the descendants of the guilty immigrants. In hauntings, he said, physiological effects "can range from sleeplessness and depression of the reactive type, to gastrointestinal upsets. Many have skin allergies—eczema, urticaria, or edema while others have respiratory problems such as chronic sinusitis, asthma, or hay fever. They seem to be illustrating the saying that 'the sorrows with their unshed tears make organs weep.'"

I heard from a woman in Newburyport, Massachusetts, who moved into a house registered as a landmark with a long history of rough sea-faring owners who seemed to haunt the place—causing many disruptions. "Antiques bought for the children as they grew would cause night-mares," she reported. "We bought a 1700's rope bed for our son. He started spiking mysterious 104-degree fevers. We were constantly rushing him to the hospital. He started telling us about the people who would come and play with him when he was sleeping. After about a year of this, we got rid of the bed, and the fevers and 'visits' stopped."

"To protect oneself from these entities, one must not invite them in your home or soul by speaking to them," emphasizes an expert. "It is very dangerous. Pray for him to find peace and forgiveness and for God and His angels to guide him to another place away from His people on earth. Remember that the God of all things loves all things equally and will never cease from helping His lost sheep find their way back home."

Many problems in family lineages, said Dr. McAll, can be traced to hidden sin. "A mother seeking help for her anorexic daughter admitted the fact of an abortion, apolo-gized to God, and in prayer committed the baby by name," wrote the psychiatrist. "Not only was the girl's anorexia healed, but the mother's constant headaches suddenly ceased. Several examples have a combined therapy, where there are family patterns of migraine. One such, a forty-year-old woman, was the fourth generation of sufferers. The proof of origin came after Confession and absolution because family members in each of the previous three generations had dabbled in the occult. Early in our inquiries we found that a number of anorexic patients had histories of one or more abortions, miscarriages, or other unmourned deaths in their immediate families," said Dr. McAll. "They recovered rapidly when the family ritually mourned these deaths. If there were signs of unresolved grief, the patient and the family were helped to look objectively at the relevance of such grief to the symptoms. Thus, they understood that these symptoms correlated with the situation of the unmourned person—that is, lost, lonely, depressed, unloved, nameless, unable to eat or cry out.

"A man of forty-eight [who had been diagnosed as having schizophrenia] was delighted that after thirty years of treatment, someone asked him for details of his halluci-nations. He explained, 'Lots of men are killing each other with swords; there is blood everywhere, a roaring sea, wind on my face, the smell of sulfur and blinding flashes.' It was discovered that he was the direct descendant of pirates and naval captains since 1580. The man was released that same evening after prayers and two days later the family attended a Requiem Mass. Through this, his brother became a priest, and the former patient is now a college lecturer."

Are there intractable problems that plague our families? Might it be financial misfortune, division, or even cancer?

Might it be traced to problems going back for genera-tions—a "haunted" family tree?

And if so, is it not wise to present our family lineages to God during the Eucharist and ask Him to break any bondage (perhaps drawing a family tree and putting a Cross between each generation)?

The spirits around us can affect our subconscious—and it is in the subconscious that we frequently detect them. Sometimes, the spiritual baggage of an entire family seems to fall on a single person. This can be because they have drawn negativity (through pride, hatred, or jealously), or were chosen to be a victim soul.

We separately discern each case but note the times when anger erupts as the possible sign of a negative pres-ence (along with too many illnesses). When we spiritually cleanse (especially ridding ourselves of anger, lust, or resentment), we are less prone to spiritual baggage. The curse does not alight (see *Proverbs* 26:2).

This cleansing is important for everyone and every place—even the Vatican.

In fact, St. Peter's Basilica was built on fill dumped on an old pagan necropolis (replete with obscene and occult relics) and at one point was so haunted by crows that an exorcism was ordered.

"In ancient times, Roman historians tell us, this swampy region beyond the Tiber was an eerie borderland of fevers and giant snakes, where the voices of the gods could be heard," reported *The Atlantic Monthly*. "These historians derived the name *Vaticanum* from *vates*, a holy seer who understood these voices."

In 1624, it was noted, Pope Urban VIII ordered that the deep foundation work for Gianlorenzo Bernini's towering bronze canopy over the high altar begin but "no sooner had ground been broken than the excavators started dropping dead," said the magazine. "Urban himself fell ill, and all Rome whispered of [a] curse."

Chapter 11

Of course, the site was cleansed and the spirits dispersed. This was standard procedure in the foundation of our Church: from the very start, pagan sites were replaced by Catholic ones, often shrines inspired by miracles of the Blessed Mother.

Catholicism's origin, then, is a history of purging evil (as this was also a mission of the Lord).

It is also our mission. Anyone who taps into evil has to purge in the end. Curses follow objects and movies and music, especially a voodoo-like "beat" or obscene lyrics. It is our guardians (and deceased loved ones) who protect us.

One day you will learn that there were many close calls with death you didn't realize at the time.

It was your guardian who whispered to you to leave a minute sooner or later (so that you would miss what would have been an accident) or guided you to the right place to meet the person who would become your spouse.

As for the deceased, they seem to be especially prevalent—along with angels—at death.

"The first shared experience reportedly was deathbed visions, most often of the dying person's mother or mother figure," noted the Los Angeles archdiocesan newspaper, which interviewed David Kessler, who runs a hospice program in California and described what the dying have told health-care workers. "Their eyes became fixed on something no one else in the room could see as they reached out their hands passionately, according to many witnesses of deathbed scenes. A hospital supervisor who Kessler calls 'Nina' in his book said her dying husband suddenly started talking to someone in his hospital room, although no one else was present. She clearly heard him say, 'Mom, I can't believe you're here.' Then he told his dead mother all about his living family. But the supervisor said the 'most amazing part' was how her husband kept his eyes focused upward on a particular spot, like his mother was hovering there. An oncologist was at the bedside of his brother, who had terminal cancer, with their mother. The patient began talking as if there was somebody right in front of him. And it soon became apparent that he was speaking to his father's parents, whom he'd been particularly close to. The conversation lasted for a couple of hours, with the patient smiling and calling both of his grandparents by name. 'As a doctor, it's very easy to dismiss this sort of thing until you see it firsthand,' the oncologist told Kessler, adding, 'Before the episode, there was a sense of struggle and tension in the air, but now there seemed to be only peace surrounding my brother. I truly believe that it was a result of my grandparents' visit as he died.' Kessler found that deathbed vision happenings shared a number of things. First, death had to be imminent, within at least a week and sometimes the same day. Only really dying people, in short, had visions. And these end-of-life visions were remarkably similar, with mothers or mother-like figures being the most likely apparitions. 'The more I thought about it, I wasn't as surprised as

I might have been [said Kessler], because our mother ushers us through this threshold into life—and wouldn't she be there at the end?'"

Many of those on their deathbeds report seeing Jesus and angels.

Many too are those who as they approach death say that there is a crowd around them—a room full of relatives and friends and acquaintances, as well as angels or other holy figures.

Remarkable are the cases whereby a person still alive encounters a person who has died—without knowing that person is dead.

This happened, according to Kessler, with an elderly woman who was dying of pancreatic cancer while her husband was at another facility for severe Alzheimer's.

As the family sat around the mom, she suddenly said, "Joseph died. Why didn't anyone tell me this?"

"Mom, daddy isn't dead," replied her daughter, a nurse named Heather. "He's still in the nursing home."

The daughter decided that it might be time to get her father over, in the event that the mother passed. "'Mom,'" I said, "'we'll see if the nursing home will let us pick up dad so he can visit.' I nodded to my cousin Jackie to call the nursing home to make arrangements for one of us to get him."

But the mother insisted that "Joseph already came to say good-bye, and he told me that I'd be with him soon."

They all looked at each other, knowing that she was in her final stages and hallucinating. When it was repeated that he was in the nursing home, the mother repeated, "No, he's dead," and then sat up exclaiming, "Look, there he is!" She seemed to be staring beyond anyone in the room and her eyes filled with tears.

"Just then, a nurse and my cousin motioned for me to come over and talk to them at the nurses' station," recalled

Heather. "I met them just outside the door when Jackie said, 'Heather, I don't know how to tell you this. I called the nursing home, and Joseph died about fifteen minutes ago. He had a heart attack.'"

The mother, he reports, died two days later.

Equal in number are reports—during death—of those guardians.

This only makes sense because they are always there. It was the guardian who "advised" you on what to eat in order to avoid a disease toward which you may have been genetically prone. When there is a special "glow" around a person, it could be an angel wrapping himself around the person, and on the other side of the veil, we'll note the way they operate. When we pray, it is like a beam of light and they delight in responding to it.

Many of us have encountered angels (guardians or otherwise) as mysterious strangers—often unusually cheerful people who suddenly appear to encourage us or help us in a circumstance (even if it's a flat tire). I have had this happen myself.

Then, they seem to walk around a corner or bend and disappear.

We all have encounters with angels, whether we realize it or not. They are closer than your shadow and have been with you since you were born. They have known you "forever" and are the reason for many of your inspired thoughts, for sudden joy, for triumphs you never expected.

They nudged you from wrong things you desired.

When we die, we'll be astonished at how many times angels interceded—and how many times we ran into them without realizing who they were.

Said one woman who had a near-death experience, "I saw that many of my experiences had been orchestrated by guardian angels. I saw that guardian angels remained with me through my trials, helping me in any way they could. Sometimes I had many guardian angels around me, sometimes just a few, depending on my needs."

She saw warring angels as "giant men, very muscularly built, with a wonderful countenance about them. They are magnificent spirits. I understood simply by looking at them that to struggle against them would be an act of futility. They were actually dressed like warriors, in headdress and armor, and I saw that they moved more swiftly than other angels. But perhaps what set them apart more than anything was their aura of confidence; they were absolutely sure of their abilities. Nothing evil could daunt them, and they knew it. As they suddenly rushed off on some mission, I was moved by their looks of concern; they understood the importance of their mission, and they knew, and I knew, that they would not return until it was accomplished."

Chapter 12

They have missions because of those negative spirits around us all. In the news just now: a pop singer had her home "exorcised" due to the ghost of a young boy who she blames for repeated bouts of tonsillitis. Just her imagination?

I mentioned the "curse" of movies and the danger of music. There was *Rosemary's Baby* (starring Mia Farrow), a movie about a woman who bears the devil's child. In this case the director's wife was murdered a year after the movie by Charlie Manson and his "family," one member of whom had been a disciple of Satanist Anton LaVey—who reportedly had been a consultant to *Rosemary's Baby*. The movie was filmed at a famous, "haunted" apartment building on the West Side of Manhattan called the Dakota. Years later, John Lennon moved there, holding psychic sessions and séances with wife Yoko Ono. He was later killed by a fan from Hawaii who heard the voice of "little people" telling him to slay Lennon.

The last person the murderer recognized before pulling the trigger was a celebrity passerby walking her dog, Mia Farrow.

We see then how life and spirits interweave and how we must root out the negative ones (without focusing too much on them). When a mystic was asked what was haunting a family, she "saw" that it was a "great-great grandfather" afflicting a youngster in that home. "I knew the spirit wasn't good for the family, that he was in some way a malevolent force, and that his presence was a part, if not all, of the child's sickness," she wrote. "All the time I was in that house I kept watching this spirit and praying that he be surrounded by love and angels, so that he could depart and go to Heaven and leave the little boy in peace."

God always helps us purge.

When we believe in the help of angels, meanwhile, it empowers them.

Surround yourself.

Misfortune, accidents, sudden emotional effect, anxiety, depression, poor luck in love, addiction, melancholy, exhaustion, and immorality can all have a root in unseen realities. There was that case of the spiritually troubled man who was very much afraid to die and kept going into a demonic rage. At one point, allegedly, nurses saw him hovering two inches above his bed. "I was supposed to be putting on a brave front for the less experienced nurses, but I'm still freaked out from that night," she said. "I quit working at that hospital not long after. Before I left, I started to notice come changes throughout the unit. There were strange sounds. Peoples' personalities were changing. I watched some of the quiet, shy nurses become very sexual or verbally abusive. We had one nurse who was a very devout Christian. I'd never heard a bad word about anyone or even a curse. She always smiled, was very polite, but after that night, she'd let out a string of curse words and obscenities that I'd never heard before and she had the same evil look in her eye as that patient did that night. That hospital needed a priest."

Many do. That isn't to blame spirits for our sins. We have free will. But brushing up against evil can affect us if we don't cast it off and we must always guard against unusual problems and temptations (as well as personality change).

Often, "temptation" is from invisible entities.

Curses can be very subtle. They can originate from anyone. Frequently they're the product of jealousy. When a person wishes poorly for you, that can have repercussions—and the same can occur when *we* do it, making it urgent that we cleanse our thoughts, thinking negatively of no one and certainly not wishing negativity upon them! It always returns. Scripture says a curse will not "alight" without cause. This emphasizes the need to purify our interior lives.

Often, spirits come in groups. There is more than one. This makes it hard to discern. In Mandaluyong City, Philippines, a young priest who went to bless a "haunted" bungalow heard a moaning sound as he was doing so with Holy Water and was told that housemaids who looked after an elderly man there were spooked and always left after a few days—claiming to see slippers or even chairs move by themselves.

It turned out that as a younger man this person held occult sessions with a Ouija board and that the guests had been wealthy folks—many of whom later suffered bankruptcy or tragic deaths.

One was a well-know socialite whose mysterious murder made headlines.

A "man" with "horns and a tail" was seen behind the elderly Filipino, in this case, as if watching television with him.

Confession beforehand, and fasting, are important in such cases. The Hour of Mercy is an excellent time to pray.

Crucifixes over every door are wise, along with the pictures of the Sacred and Immaculate Hearts (especially near the entrance). *This declares that the house belongs to God.* Praising Him weakens evil attack. Never use a talisman such as the "horns" or pepper pendant employed by some Italians to ward off evil forces. *These actually can attract them.* "If the [occupants of the home] should happen to make use of superstitious means condemned by the Church to rid themselves of the curse, they enter, though without knowing it perhaps, into communication with the powers of darkness, which then acquire fresh strength," said a famed mystic, Blessed Anne Catherine Emmerich. A way of thinking that is full of love and non-judgmental is the safest route, in combination with the Rosary. It is important for us to keep ourselves and our homes *clear*. The Blessed Mother helps poor souls—and chases away demonic ones. Fasting potentiates prayer and reading the Bible—even just leaving it open (especially to *Ephesians* 6, or *Psalms* 21)—can help deter attacks. Jesus indicated that spirits come in groups when He cast numerous ones from a man into swine and removed seven spirits from Mary Magdalene and also when He explained how a spirit can return with other ones: "Then it goes and takes along with it seven other spirits more wicked than itself, and they go in and live there; and the last state of that man becomes worse than the first," says *Matthew* 12:45.

Thus we must cast out the main or "root" spirit in order to dispel a group. It is the Holy Spirit Who leads us into how we must phrase our prayers for deliverance.

The reference to pigs—and spirits entering them—raises the issue of animals and here we are on delicate—if fascinating—ground.

We touched on this with Balaam. Can spirits possess animals? There are certainly aspects of spiritual phenomena that seem fringe—and certainly beyond common belief.

Dogs often howl when their masters die—even if the death occurs at a distance. Animals seem to sense spiritual presences—whether dogs, cats, birds, or whatever, often looking strangely to a corner of a room, or becoming flustered. In the *Life of St. Hilarion* it's stated that the saint often dealt with furious animals possessed by demons. "One day there was brought to him an enormous camel which had killed several persons," noted a famous demonologist named Father Delaporte in a classical work called *The Devil*. "It was dragged along by more than thirty men, with great ropes; its eyes were bloodshot, its mouth frothing, its tongue swollen and constantly moving; its frightful roaring filled the air with a strange and dismal sound." Hilarion addressed the spirit with derision. "Whether thou art in a fox or a camel, thou art always the same," he said. "Thou dost not frighten me." With that the animal tried to charge him but suddenly fell to the ground.

At times, it is as if angels take over an animal to save a human life (one priest told me how his mastiff literally dragged him out of his bed when a gas pipe sprung a leak while he was sleeping), and in other cases it seems evil. In Liberia, an elephant thought to be possessed by human spirits was killed after trampling a logging employee. For some reason, elephants have been prominent in this regard—particularly in India, where they seemed to avenge violence against Christians. "In July 2008, a severe persecution of Christians broke out in the Indian state of Orissa," wrote a priest there, Father Sunil De Silva. "A 22-year-old nun was burnt to death when angry mobs burnt down an orphanage in Khuntpali village in Barhgarh district. Another nun was gang raped in Kandhamal. Mobs attacked churches, torched vehicles, and houses of Christians have been destroyed. Father Thomas Chellen, director of a pastoral center destroyed by a bomb, had a narrow escape after a Hindu mob nearly set him on fire. The end result saw more than five hundred Christians murdered, and thousands of others injured and homeless after their houses were reduced to ashes.

"[But] recently a strange and dramatic event took place, which has many people talking and wondering. In Orissa, herds of wild elephants have begun to storm villages that are home to some of the worst persecutors of Christians during the troubles. In one village, where Christians had to run for their lives while their homes were being destroyed by rioters, a herd of elephants emerged from the surrounding jungle exactly one year later, in July 2009, at the same time as the day of the attack. These elephants first attacked a rock crusher machine owned by a key leader of the persecution movement. They then went on to destroy his house and farms."

It is said by some that spirits especially enter birds, and we think here of the doves that uncannily nest at Assisi in the arms of a statue of St. Francis. Ravens and crows are known at strange moments to congregate around cemeteries. In Japan a blaze was sparked when they picked up incense from a graveyard and dropped it on a forest nearby. At a Church-approved apparition spot in Betania, Venezuela, a blue butterfly was known to flit from a Lourdes grotto at the moment of apparition. "The saints who have received private revelations from Mary, Mother of Jesus, tell us that on occasion, the Blessed Mother is seen with a bird or birds about her," says author Susi Pittman. "I have had personal experiences at the death of some of my animals that indicate the miraculous."

From *Ecclesiastes* 3:21: "Who knows whether the spirit of man goes upward and the spirit of the beast goes down to the earth?"

In Australia, the death of a dad was marked by an unusual, V-shaped flock of birds on the day of the funeral.

"A few days after the 9-11 attacks, I was driving from home in Lebanon, Indiana, to Indianapolis," said a woman named Cindy Thrine. "As I drove, I thought about the attacks and about my concerns for our country's future. For some time I had been praying for America to return to being 'one nation under God.' As I talked with God about my concerns, a large flock of birds caught my eye as they flew in the sky. There had to be hundreds of birds flying slowly together. It looked like a ribbon flowing in a breeze as the flock dipped and soared in the sky. Suddenly I was overwhelmed as the birds' flight took the shape of a huge heart in the sky. I smiled and silently thanked God for his love and for displaying his presence in my life."

In many cases, the animals are spectral. "Yet again there is high-strangeness afoot in the woods of Britain's Cannock Chase and specifically in the vicinity of its German cemetery," noted a blogger. "The cemetery in question has been a veritable hotbed of weirdness for years: bigfoot, werewolves, hairy sprites, ghosts, marauding black cats, and spectral black dogs have all been seen roaming amongst the old war graves. Now there's a new player in town: a giant snake that has been slithering around the area."

There is no doubt that animals figure into glimpses of the other side in alleged near-death episodes as well as stark dreams. "My beloved dog Zack died of cancer in January, 2004," penned a viewer named Ellen from Matthew, North Carolina. "His previous owners had abused him, so he didn't like to be touched on his head. When he got sick, he started sidling up to the couch where I was sitting, leaning against me for a comforting touch, and then would walk away. Two weeks after he died, I came home from work early due to illness and rested on the couch. Somewhere in between that time of awake and sleep, I saw Zack coming toward me. There was a liquidity to his appearance. He sidled up to the couch so I could pet him for the last time. Then he walked away and was gone. I believe the Lord let Zack come back to let me know he was okay and to also comfort others with this story. God is so good!"

In Colorado a perfect profile of a Labrador retriever materialized in startling detail on the grill cover of a family who just lost such a pet.

Chapter 13

We can take this all into discernment but must know that the vast majority of spiritual experiences are human.

And more than anything, they relate to family lines.

In the afterlife, as also here on earth, families are critical—going all the way back to Adam. And going all that way, there are areas of darkness. To pray this darkness out of our familial lineage is a task of life. Those who have near-death experiences have described being met on the other side by thousands of souls they didn't know but who turned out to be ancestors—thrilled to greet the newcomer. Sometimes, in such descriptions, the relatives even erupt in applause—as if to indicate that the person had accomplished something for the entire family line in the tests of earth.

As a deliverance minister once said: "Confess the sins of your ancestors (*Nehemiah* 1:5, 6 and *Daniel* 9:4-12, 16-19), asking God at the same time to nullify the effect of those sins upon your family line. If you suspect an ancestral curse, by faith nullify its power over you. Any legal right or hold that Satan might have over your life because of the sins of your ancestors needs to be cancelled out through the proper exercise of spiritual authority."

"The Holy Spirit reveals mysteries," wrote another expert, Father Robert DeGrandis. "The whole topic of inheritance is a great mystery, yet I believe if we allow the Spirit of God to teach us, He will reveal some more pieces of the puzzle. I believe He will also show us to use the information to bring healing and wholeness beyond our imaginations." He quotes Father Hampsch as adding: "Families are the building blocks of society; as basic natural social clusters they have a very special place in God's Plan of corporate sanctions. Because families are constituted by the sacred union of matrimony, they fall in a special way under His sanctions. The frequent blessings of the Old Testament on God-reverencing families make this clear with regard to external things such as wealth, social status, and even health. But even more importantly, the things that are internal to the family reflect the family members' allegiance to God and His Law. Thus when a family strives to live together in praise and thanksgiving and trust, its members will know contentment and harmony. If they are negligent or disobedient in these areas, they will experience God's judgment negatively by the presence of domestic strife, jealousy, infidelity, suspicion, unhappiness, marital discord, broken marriages, recalcitrance in children, arguments, addictions, in-law conflicts, and so forth."

According to these priests, later generations may experience the force of the judgment that was levied upon an earlier generation. If the subsequent generations choose to repeat the patterns of their parents, or ancestors, they assume responsibility not only individually but also corporately for what had been done earlier. Even one member of a family can be the means of salvation for a whole family.

Ax the roots that dark spirits use as conduits, and miracles will happen.

Otherwise, we may be prone even to tragedies.

"The prayer to break the transgenerational bondage must not only interrupt the 'flow' of that deleterious effect, but must also go further and release the very *persons themselves*—not only those who are alive, but also and especially those who are deceased—in the event that they may be in need of deliverance from any lingering effects in themselves of their own sins," claims Father Hampsch. "The needs that these persons sometimes have can come to us in indirect ways, such as through dreams or through an awareness of a disquieted spirit in our environment, even by apparitional phenomena (somewhat rare), or it may be by a simple spiritual intuition of a deceased person's need in one's family background.

"Wherever there is any attachment to sin (intrinsic evil) there is usually an attempt of the extrinsic forces, demonic forces, to lodge in those areas. But Jesus, Who says, 'The prince of this world has no power over Me' (*John* 14:30), should be called upon to cleanse the bloodlines of the family tree, both living and dead, of anything of evil that may block the healthy state of the individuals within that family. Through Jesus' Power we can break any inherited curses or hexes that may have been transmitted through the generations, and cast out any evil spirits that may harass the living members of the family." This is most effectively done, he maintains, through the Eucharist.

The steps to healing: recognizing the issues, repenting of all failures, forgiving all members of a family (including ancestors), praying for deliverance of the lineage, true conversion (separating oneself from worldliness), sending the deceased to the Light, appealing for the aid of angels, and—again—placing the Cross of Jesus between each of the generations and over the head of each member of the family who comes to mind in a special fashion. Evict spirits of adultery, addiction, atheism, or any sinful pattern. Replace fallen angels that have congregated with holy ones. Persevere.

And to this I would add: have no fear.

To have fear is to have faith in the power of the negative, which unfortunately empowers it further. That was made plain to me one time when I was speaking at a large church in the Chicago area and spending the night in a former convent. The convent, large and dark, had been abandoned, it turned out, due to division among the sisters that some traced as coming from practices of the "New Age." It is a huge problem in our time: the involvement of nuns with the occult, including at retreat centers. At any rate: I heard strange sounds while getting ready for bed, and for a few minutes let fear grip me—all the while noticing the sounds becoming louder (until I heard actual footsteps). Only when I took hold of myself and prayed a Rosary did the sounds stop (and then I had a very restful sleep, not even giving it much thought the next morning).

As far back as the sixth century, Pope Gregory the Great logged afterlife accounts, including those of spirits at public baths—spirits that vanished once devout prayers were offered for them. For centuries, ghostly accounts were reported by prominent clergy. Noted Saxon Bishop Theitmar of Merseburg (975-1018), "It is not right and proper to dwell too much upon the affairs of the dead, but rather, as St. Paul reminds us (*Romans* 12:3) to think soberly upon such matters. On the other hand, because the testimony of two or three witnesses is worth recording, I have written down accounts of events which have happened recently, in order that the unbelieving might know that the words of the prophets are true: 'Thy dead shall live, O Lord' (*Isaiah* 26:19, and also 'The dead arise, who are in their tombs; they will hear the voice of the Son of God, and abundantly' (*John* 5:28)." Continued this ancient bishop: "It is noteworthy that, whenever such events occur and are witnessed by the living, they signify that something momentous is about to happen. For instance, I was myself in my courtyard one December when, as the cock crowed, a great light came from the church, filling the whole of the atrium, and an immense sound—a kind of groaning—was heard. My brother witnessed this with his attendants and others who were gathered there, and a chaplain sleeping nearby heard the sounds.

"When I asked the next day whether similar phenomena had occurred in the past, I learned from some old men that they had; and, sad to say, shortly afterwards there was a fulfillment of these events with the death of my niece and kinswoman. It often happened that during the night I heard the sound of timbers being cut down, and on one occasion I and a companion became aware, as others slept, of the dead speaking to one another. By these signs I would learn of the imminence of another death."

However "far" away, relatives are always close to us— able to reach into our realm when God allows.

Wrote a woman named Jessica Stefanow of Lebanon, Pennsylvania, "I just wanted to let you know about two experiences that I've had since my grandmother (to whom I was very close) passed away in 1996. She had given me an antique doll that played the piano when you opened a drawer in the front. It hadn't worked for years, needed to be fixed. On the day of her funeral, this doll played by itself for about five or ten seconds. My mom and I just looked at each other in shock! It didn't play another note for almost ten years, when I finally found someone who could repair it! The second experience: I bought the house that my grandma lived (and died) in about five years after she passed away. In the eight years I've lived here, I often will smell her perfume (which was a very distinct scent), especially in my sons' room (it was her bedroom) and in the hallway. Every time I do, I feel so peaceful and happy. I feel like she's just letting me know that she's watching over us."

"A number of years ago my husband abandoned our family and moved to Kansas City to live with another woman," recalled another witness, Donna M. Giberti. "In the midst of the turbulence, many life-changing hardships occurred. Every day for over five years I prayed for him and said the Rosary. I asked the Blessed Virgin to be with him as his mother and to intercede for me, helping him to know and love God. I prayed to the Lord, asking Him to one day reveal to me what had become of my husband's life and knowledge about whether his soul had been rescued.

"Three years after my husband left I began to powerfully experience feelings of his presence, especially in the quiet of the evenings," continued Donna. "I couldn't imagine why this was happening since I had worked hard to move through the grief process and was doing well. Oftentimes he seemed so close that I thought if I looked into the mirror, I might see him standing behind me. I recall exclaiming out loud, 'Why does it feel as though you're right here when I know you're two thousand miles away?' During a period spanning two years, I would sometime sense a strong urgency to locate him through the internet. Each time I resisted because all I wanted was to move on with my life. I simply continued to pray for him.

"Five years after our separation, I learned, through a third party and an extremely odd series of circumstances that my husband *had died two years earlier*, at the young age of 43. His death coincided with the same time that I had begun to feel his presence with me. I received news of his death on August 15—feast of the Assumption of Mary into Heaven, which I took as a sign that she had heard my prayers and had been with him on his journey to eternal life. After learning about his passing, some of the loose ends that he had left behind came together. I was able to procure a death certificate and put things in order. Shortly afterwards, I realized that his strong presence was no longer with me. Rather than the urgency that I sensed from him before, I was now washed in a sense of peace that seemed to be saying, 'Thank you for your prayers. Now that I know everything's been set right and you'll be okay, I can move on.'"

"In April of 1984 my late husband, Tom, died of Hodgkin's lymphoma at the young age of 24," adds Cindy Schwenk Accetta Dodge of Midlothian, Virginia. "Our children were two years and three months old at the time. A few weeks earlier he was rushed to emergency surgery at Duke University Medical Center with pericardial effusion from which he never recovered.

"The last few words spoken between us took place as they were rushing him to surgery. We didn't get a chance to say goodbye or 'I love you.' Frankly we didn't understand how gravely ill he was. From surgery to the time of his death, family surrounded his bedside. He was able to write a few words on paper to our priest and to the nurses. It was the first time I had ever prayed the Rosary. I shared Holy Eucharist with him as the priest broke the single host and offered Tom the slightest speck of the Eucharist and allowed me to receive the remaining body of the Lord.

"I knew the instant Tom left his body because I felt a swift and powerful wave pass through me. About ten seconds later his heart beat flat-lined on the monitor. Strange events started happening after that. My lights would turn off and on in my apartment. My television would turn on and start changing channels. I would get in my car and those lights would start flashing. Frankly, I was quite frightened as I didn't understand what was happening. I was so frightened that my priest would call me at night and pray with me over the phone to help bring me some peace. Eventually I just yelled out, 'Tom if you are doing this please stop. I'm really frightened. I forgive you if you feel as though you have offended me in any way. Please forgive me too if I have ever offended you in any way.' I never again had problems with the television or lighting again."

At times the manifestations are–allegedly—spectacular.

In Australia, mysterious oil began to seep from the bedroom walls of a seventeen-year-old who died in a car accident.

Was it real?

At times of special challenges, God allows souls of the departed to make themselves a bit more apparent or sends angels—never in a way that subverts the need for faith, never in a scientific "proof," but in a way that elevates the spirit.

Or, because there is an emergency.

A life lived as a strict Catholic (but one that is non-judgmental and always open to love) is the safest way to Heaven.

Watch that you never obsess. Watch over-attachments. Clear yourself of imbalance. Ask Jesus every day what you need to do to form the best afterlife.

He will guide you as to what steps you need to take toward *perfection*.

Don't think you can't reach that. Don't believe for a moment that you're "too far away."

No matter what you have done or "failed to do," purification is often the short step to simply giving everything to Jesus.

Call out constantly for His Spirit. Do His Will. Let unconditional love encompass your every thought of everyone.

Never judge and you will find happiness because you will no longer find the need for anger.

With unconditional affection, there is no irritation—not long-lasting, anyway.

Every difficulty is simply a challenge, and every time it is overcome with love, it is in your riches afterward.

Keep yourself clean on earth, and remember all the traps. An example is tattoos: an emblem of evil can draw evil.

I recall an article by a Catholic deliverance minister who was tending to a young woman named Jody. This woman had strange pains in her legs and was also contemplating suicide.

"The day she arrived, two other prayer team members and myself were ready to pray healing for her legs," wrote this minister. "We began with praising Jesus, then prayed the prayer of protection and bound any spirits not in worship to the Trinity. We invited Jesus to be present during our healing session. Jody lay on a table, and we began applying blessed oil for healing on her legs. The three of us were praying for her and praying in tongues. As the blessing in the oil touched her skin, large goose bumps formed. Her body temperature dropped, as if she had a spirit of death. We prayed the death spirit of suicide to leave her. She manifested a few times, and it was gone. After we put the blessed oil on the front of her legs, she turned, so we could pray over the back of her legs. There it was! The tattoo! On her lower leg and heel was the tattoo of a dragon!"

In the news is a young man in England who broke his neck in a crash right after receiving the tattoo of an angel. He figured the tattoo saved his life. However, the "angel" looked more like a fairy.

The same can enter when a teenager has posters of heavy-metal rockers giving the devil's salute (those two fingers) or clad in spiked leather.

Did you ever notice that the finger salute is usually seen at various events where there is a frenzy (or something questionable behind the event to start with)?

The devil is clever and wants us to think such things are innocuous but they are not and he attacks in emotional breakdown or repeated chronic sickness or in barrenness (a tendency to miscarry) or in the breakdown of families or in continuing financial insufficiency or in a family history of unnatural or untimely deaths or in being accident or injury prone. When someone thinks negatively of us, they can be sending the negative spirits—telegraphing them with unknown consequences. To dispel that, we ask the Lord to first search our own spirits for darkness and then pray to build a bubble of protection around us. This is best done through love. Humble yourself, confess any known sin, repent of all transgressions, forgive other people, break with anything remotely occult, and also forgive yourself—release yourself from what haunted you in your past, and may still haunt your conscience (keeping you bound).

Then, take your place as a child of the Almighty One and expel any darkness!

Breathe it right out.

Seal yourself with the Holy Spirit.

Surround yourself with angels.

These are not just tools of the mind. They are actions that bring *power*.

When one man encountered his deceased wife, she allegedly said, "I have forgiven you. Now you need to forgive yourself, so I can move on."

When we don't forgive we may hold back ourselves and hold down those who have gone before us. Most of all, get rid of pride. It blocks love. Said one famous deliverance expert, "If we approach God with an attitude of pride, He resists us and we have no access to Him. So our first step toward God must be to humble ourselves, to say to God, 'I need You!'"

The responsibility is ours!

Humble yourself. Take your stand with God. Break all curses. Pray for ancestors back to Adam. Here is one prayer offered by Father Hampsch:

"Heavenly Father, I come before you as your child, in great need of your help; I have physical health needs, emotional needs, spiritual needs, and interpersonal needs. Many of my problems have been caused by my own failures, neglect and sinfulness, for which I humbly beg your forgiveness, Lord. But I also ask you to forgive the sins of my ancestors whose failures have left their effects on me in the form of unwanted tendencies, behavior patterns and defects in body, mind and spirit. Heal me, Lord, of all these disorders.

"With your help I sincerely forgive everyone, especially living or dead members of my family tree, who have directly offended me or my loved ones in any way, or those whose sins have resulted in our present sufferings and disorders. In the name of your divine Son, Jesus, and in the power of his Holy Spirit, I ask you, Father, to deliver me and my entire family tree from the influence of the evil one. Free all living and dead members of my family tree, including those in adoptive relationships, and those in extended family relationships, from every contaminating form of bondage. By your loving concern for us, heavenly Father, and by the shed blood of your precious Son, Jesus, I beg you to extend your blessing to me and to all my living and deceased relatives. Heal every negative effect transmitted through all past generations, and prevent such negative effects in future generations of my family tree.

"I symbolically place the cross of Jesus over the head of each person in my family tree, and between each generation; I ask you to let the cleansing blood of Jesus purify the bloodlines in my family lineage. Set your protective angels to

encamp around us, and permit Archangel Raphael, the patron of healing, to administer your divine healing power to all of us, even in areas of genetic disability. Give special power to our family members' guardian angels to heal, protect, guide and encourage each of us in all our needs. Let your healing power be released at this very moment, and let it continue as long as your sovereignty permits.

"In our family tree, Lord, replace all bondage with a holy bonding in family love. And let there be an ever-deeper bonding with you, Lord, by the Holy Spirit, to your Son, Jesus. Let the family of the Holy Trinity pervade our family with its tender, warm, loving presence, so that our family may recognize and manifest that love in all our relationships. All of our unknown needs we include with this petition that we pray in Jesus' precious Name. Amen.

"St. Joseph, Patron of family life, pray for us."

Chapter 14

And now we are on the way to freedom.

There is nothing like freedom in the spirit!

When we expel the demonic, we feel a flow of peace. We approach a sense of well-being.

There can be so many spirits in or around us.

Remember that when Jesus cast unclean ones out of those two in the region of the Gadarenes (*Matthew* 8), they took over a whole herd of pigs.

They were "legion."

They kept the one man (*Mark* 5) in a cemetery.

Note that he lived among the tombs!

Note too how he tried to hurt himself.

Without prayer, we have no shield.

Prayer in our homes prevents negative revenants.

How many minor manifestations do we suffer from unseen realities around us—and more to the point, how often have they fired our emotions? How do they affect our relationships? How do they affect our health? Spirits sometimes "take our breath away" (see origin of the word pneumonia, from *pneuma*, the blow of the wind, breath, and soul-heart, or spirit, in ancient Greek).

Of course, not all spirits are bad.

St. John Bosco once made a pact with a fellow student named Comollo: whoever died first would try to communicate to the other the state of his own soul. The student died on April 2, 1839, and the next night, following the funeral, St. Bosco sat waiting on his bed in a dormitory that had twenty other seminarians. "Midnight struck, and I then heard a dull, rolling sound from the end of the passage," recounted the saint. "While the noise came nearer the dormitory, the walls, ceiling and floor of the passage re-echoed and trembled behind it. The students in the dormitory awoke, but none of them spoke. Then the door opened violently of its own accord without anybody seeing anything except a dim light of changing color that seemed to control the sound. Then a voice was clearly heard. 'Bosco, Bosco, Bosco, I am saved.' The seminarists leapt out of bed and fled without knowing where to go.

"All had heard the noise and some of them the voice without gathering the meaning of the words."

Added Father Dominic Legge, a theologian at Providence College who penned the item for a Catholic website called Headline Bistro, operated by the Knights of Columbus: "In the middle of the night at a large, old, and now only partly occupied Dominican priory in rural Ohio, a Dominican woke up to see an unknown man, wearing the white habit of the order, standing at the foot of his bed, looking at him. The figure pointed insistently at the bookcase against the wall, and then *turned and walked out of the room.* After breakfast the next morning, the friar took aside the superior of the house. 'One of our guests walked into my room last night. It was very strange.' 'What guest?' the prior replied. 'The visiting Dominican—someone I didn't recognize. He came into my room in the middle of the night.' 'But we don't have any guests staying with us,' the prior insisted. 'You must have been dreaming.' 'I don't think so.'

"When he returned to his room, he studied the bookcase: nothing unusual there. He peered behind it, moved it a few inches. Intrigued, he now strained to pivot the bookcase away from the wall. A forgotten door, unopened for decades, stood before him.

"The door opened; the friar peered into a dusty closet containing a bureau. Inside the bureau, he found a stack of yellowed slips of paper: Mass intentions. Some priest had long ago left these promises to say Mass for the souls of the dead without fulfilling them. Perhaps that is why the unknown Dominican desired so much that these papers be found—so that the duty he had failed to fulfill in his life could be completed by his brothers who remained alive.

"The room was turned into a chapel, an altar erected. Many Masses were offered there. The unknown Dominican never appeared again."

Chapter 15

The accounts go on. Alas, one can not include them all. And indeed, many of the well-known ones have to do with a nun or monk or priest returning or sending signs.

Perhaps holy clergy have a special privilege or simply that the veil is thinner around those consecrated to God.

As far back as 1965, CBS aired a special that included the photograph of monks walking as "stately ghosts" at the site of an old monastery, visible only from their knees up; later it was learned that centuries before, the monastery had been a couple of feet lower. (The documentary, narrated by Walter Cronkite, was called, "The Stately Ghosts of England.")

Monks. Nuns. Images. In Santiago, Chile, visitors flocked to see what clearly seemed like the full figure of a priest holding a child on a wall at Christo Rey de Tome Church (presumed to be a deceased cleric who because of his work with needy children is due for canonization). Heavy rockers who used a converted nunnery for a studio in England were spooked by the uncanny sound of hymn-singing. In that same country some claim to see the face of another priest on the binding of a 17th-century book that dealt with his execution. In Serbia, a doctor had a recurring dream about a beautiful field full of young people from four to twenty-four years old who were playing and laughing but ran from the doctor when he approached (the doctor had committed 48,000 abortions). In the dream was also a man dressed in a white and black habit who silently stared at him.

The dream replayed each night and each night the doctor woke up in a cold sweat.

When he asked the man in white and black who he was, the vision replied, "My name is Thomas Aquinas" and explained that the children were those the doctor had aborted.

There are good presences; there are evil ones—even in houses of worship—perhaps *especially* in holy places, as revenants go there in search of prayer. In St. Augustine, floor tiles suddenly flew upward and there was a "wicked, groaning sound" at Prince of Peace Church (in the oldest part of this oldest city).

Or they may be sending a message. Well-known is the alleged case of a haunted rectory at what was once St. Charles Borromeo church in Chicago, a case intriguing because so many reliable witnesses—priests, along with an auxiliary bishop—reported spectacular phenomena. "Suddenly and without warning," says Rocco A. Facchini, a former priest who lived in the rectory and wrote a book about it, "a loud and thunderous explosion shattered the stillness. I heard what sounded like a locomotive crashing through the first-floor kitchen. The building shook violently, as if the entire rectory had been lifted off its foundation and dropped with a big bang. The walls moved and quivered, the furniture moved. Lights flickered off and then on again."

Three others in the rectory heard the disturbance, including the pastor, who long had known the revenant.

Legend had it that a deceased bishop was either upset that his ring had never been returned to his beloved parish, was trying to clear his name (he once had been wrongly implicated in a scandal), or was bothered by the current pastor's attentiveness to worldliness instead of spirituality. On one occasion, Facchini passed the room of another priest and found it open but dark inside. He headed up the hall and when he returned the lights were ablaze in the room and the radio was filling the air with classical music even though the priest had not yet returned. Searching for clues on the third floor, another pastor geared with the tools of exorcism (purple stole, Holy Water, and the *Rituale Romanum*) discovered a pyx with six old, yellowed hosts in a suit pocket. After he properly dissolved them in water and poured it into a sacarium, the disturbances stopped—for a period. But subsequent sounds were to such an extent as to convince even the most skeptical of priests who stayed there.

While, as we have seen, the Church actually takes no position on ghosts (neither accepting nor rejecting), and many prominent clerics have reported such happenings, or ministered to those who are haunted, through the centuries, Catholicism is understandably vague—and cautious—about a vague subject.

"In Christian belief, the resting place of the conscious afterlife is either Heaven for those who have achieved salvation, hell for those who are eternally damned, or purgatory for those who have died with sin and are being cleansed before entering into the Kingdom of God," wrote Facchini. "It's my belief that a ghost has not achieved any of these goals. The spirit, for some inexplicable reason, has not yet found peace in this life and continues to be bound to its earthly home."

"I've been experiencing lost souls since I was a child," says Lisa Marie Garcia of California. "When I say lost souls, though, I don't exactly mean those in purgatory. I mean those stuck here. Jesus tells us to pray always and keep our thoughts turned to God for a *good* reason. 'Where your treasure is, there your heart shall be . . .' If our hearts are on earthly things, we can get stuck here. Neither in Heaven, nor in hell, but stuck in a sort of limbo, unable to be seen or to interact with those whom we loved so much that we passed up the Light of God to remain with them."

This is controversial stuff. Whatever the case, we always lovingly pray for souls to go to the Lord, and we must be careful not to obsess about them. Aquinas said apparitions come from purgatory. At Medjuorje, the Blessed Mother was quoted as stating that when it comes to souls, *"it happens that God permits them to manifest themselves in different ways, close to their relatives on earth, in order to remind men of the existence of purgatory and to solicit their prayers to come close to God Who is just but good."*

Adds Lisa: "I have an early memory of waking up one bright morning to find a soldier sitting on my bed. He was clutching his rifle as if it were a lifeline. He said he was lost and someone said that I could help him. I understood immediately that he needed prayer to attain Heaven. So we prayed. I believe I fell asleep sometime during the prayers. When I woke up again, the soldier was gone. Perhaps I dreamed it. More recently, I read an account of some spectral monks who inhabited a golf course north of where I live. I felt a driving need to pray for them. Weeks and a lot of prayers later, I was in Adoration at a Dominican cloister and I saw them come down the aisle, one by one, finally at peace. They did not acknowledge me in any way. They simply walked past me toward the Blessed Sacrament: eight, maybe ten of them. All I could do was cry as they walked by. I believe they were Dominican. And I believe they were murdered. I know they are in Heaven now, praying for me! There are times too when one experiences the memory of death—not a soul, but only a sort of recording in the very fabric of our world. I experienced a man's death at Alcatraz Island: the purported 'haunted cell' is not haunted at all. His soul has long since moved on, but the *memory* of his death remains."

We see where we can bring relief. We see where we can clear the air. We see that we may affect an area. "Earthbound spirits don't eat or sleep, but they need energy," asserted the Catholic woman from Ohio I had previously quoted. "If you have one in a house, you are going to have an energy drain. Adults will end up with headaches, ear, nose, throat, sinus, or upper respiratory distress, because that's their weakest point. Visitors have long held that museum artifacts (in particular items from the *Titanic* or Egyptian tombs) have eerie events attached to them. "Guards, visitors, and even the police have all reported experiencing strange phenomena such as seeing apparitions," said one exhibition organizer in Britain.

They are seen especially in the haze between consciousness and unconsciousness. When Charles Lindbergh was making his historic flight, he famously claimed that "phantoms" helped him by "conversing and advising" in the cockpit (he said he actually saw vaguely outlined forms, which were transparent). Climbers on Mount Everest have long reported encounters with "spirits." When famed explorer Sir Edmund Hillary was in Antarctica, he claimed to have seen the apparition of another explorer, Ernest Shackleton, who'd died there years before. In 1967, the *American Journal of Psychiatry* described a mine disaster during which two men (one Lutheran, one Catholic) in Pennsylvania claimed to have seen Pope John XXIII in the cave alongside them, dressed in papal garb and leading them to believe they would be saved (which they were, after fourteen days).

Chapter 16

When we die, we will see that the supernatural wove in and out of everything and everyone we knew. We'll be astonished at how many times angels and other spirits were around us and how many times we ran into them without realizing who or what they were. On earth, we operate with blinders. Imagine what Jesus could see! If it seems like there are spirits everywhere, there are.

In our lives on earth, they softly whisper to our intuitions.

When they are heard, it is usually just barely perceptible (so that the test of faith remains and so as not to infringe on free will).

In our time, spirits are especially prevalent. It is a sign of the times. It is portentous.

What kind of an effect have they had?

However one may discern that, we test the spirits by calling on the Lord and Blessed Mother to be our intermediaries.

Praising God causes negative entities to back away—praising God in the Name of Jesus. If there are evil spirits around a person, without protection they can be "sent" to us if the person wishes us wrong (it is known as a "curse"). A series of negative events should open our eyes to the possibility and draw us into prayer.

We sense them more than we "encounter" them. Most of those ways, like most of our interactions with angels, are "just below the radar" of regular consciousness.

When we say "spirits," we usually think in terms of two kinds, demons and angels. Sometimes, we think of saints (hopefully often).

We avoid demons when we purify—when we get rid of anger, pride, jealousy, lust, and hatefulness.

When we do that, they have nothing to which they can "attach."

Meditate on the manifestations of pride and ego.

What we have inside is projected as a call to light or dark.

However, don't attribute a spirit to every problem. There are always doubts. It is complicated. More than one spirit may be at work—or none at all (just the workings of life).

But they are probably around more than most people imagine and may even try to incite your passions in order to draw power from it. They can be like parasites. They may weaken. It is why their presence exhausts. Out of the blue, they may flash a wave of anger and cause you the temptation of fighting with your spouse, then revel in it. They may come with an occult show on TV. They may arrive with pornography. They may come due to unforgiveness. They may draw from illicit sex. They make life seem to have no meaning. They cause malaise. They will unnerve you with suspicion. They will generate unkind thoughts. They will make you think the worst about a person or cause you to imagine insults. They may make you hear something that was not said. The earthbound do this because misery loves company and they wish to provoke fear or a tantrum while demons know how to do nothing else but cause us distress (it is their only "entertainment"). They will blind you to the workings of God.

We counter all that with purification.

Through prayer, through Mass, through Confession, through Adoration, through reading the Bible, through fasting, through the Rosary, we can purge all dark elements until we can *feel* inner cleanliness—purification, which is a shield against invasion. The Holy Spirit will guide you. It is joy. It is to taste the infinite. It is clarity. Once you feel you have cleansed your interior (that there is no longer the predominance of pride or lust or anger, no longer an inclination to criticize, no longer a want for too much of one thing, no longer a feeling toward anyone of antagonism, no longer any feeling whatsoever of gossip or revenge), then work at purifying your surroundings.

Pray that any deceased who may be clinging to your family be sent to the Light.

In the Name of Jesus, command this (only in His Name).

Clear the air of souls by offering Masses for them— whether or not you know who it might be. Ask the Blessed Mother to "clean house," since she can see what you cannot (and since she is an expert at the immaculate).

Use Holy Water and blessed salt on a regular basis. Use anointed oil. Search your home for anything that can bring darkness. Clear every room in your home, and then also outside. Sprinkle Holy Water around the house, especially across doors and windows and corners. Spirits often enter through them, though they are non-physical. Put a barrier across your thresholds. In the Name of Jesus, cast off anything that may be on your property, and do this until you can "see" clearly (and a feeling of tranquility returns).

For spirits of darkness try to *overshadow* us.

It is the negative forces with which we wrestle—those along with our flesh. We see in Scripture that it was the

Sadducees who believed neither in angels or spirits. Don't follow them. Follow the apostles. As Saint Paul said (*Ephesians* 6: 10-18): "Be strong in the Lord and in His mighty power. Put on the full armor of God so that you can take your stand against the devil's schemes. For our struggle is not against flesh and blood, but against the rulers, against the authorities, against the powers of this dark world and against the spiritual forces of evil in the heavenly realms. Therefore put on the full armor of God, so that when the day of evil comes, you may be able to stand your ground, and after you have done everything, to stand. Stand firm then, with the belt of truth buckled around your waist, with the breastplate of righteousness in place, and with your feet fitted with the readiness that comes from the gospel of peace. In addition to all this, take up the shield of faith, with which you can extinguish all the flaming arrows of the evil one. Take the helmet of salvation and the sword of the Spirit, which is the word of God. And pray in the Spirit on all occasions with all kinds of prayers and requests. With this in mind, be alert and always keep on praying for all the saints."

Angels always come.

For more on them, let's get back to those with deathbed visions—such as Linda Tavenner of Washington. D.C.

Explains Linda about the experiences of her husband, who approached death due to heart trouble:

"In April 1990, I was called in the middle of the night and told Earl was in great distress and dying—come quick. I arrived with one of my three sons and we were taken aside. A doctor began telling us they had done everything they could but that my husband was dead. He said to please wait a few minutes as they cleaned him up and then we could go in and see him. I obeyed and went to a room to begin calling family. My son did not! He went into the room and saw his father, clearly dead. The staff was unhooking the many things they'd been using to try to help him. My son noted his father was without a doubt gone, but something prompted him to blurt out, 'God, if you have ever heard a prayer of mine, please hear this one. I pray, please let my father live!

"In a few seconds he saw some movement or breathing. He called the nurses and doctor and said 'something is happening—do something for him!' They said, 'No, he is gone; it's just sometimes people have a movement or quiver after death.' My son said, 'No! Hook him back up!' In the meantime I had called my pastor to come to pray for my 'dead' husband. He came even though my husband was not Catholic. By the time he got there, the doctors were working on Earl and not believing but trying to satisfy my son's demands. Then there was a very slight pulse but no blood pressure registered for one and a half hours! I told the priest, 'Earl is alive; go in and baptize him;' and he answered 'okay.'

"That was the beginning of a recovery that was amazing. The doctors were astonished and the nurses were coming in and saying, 'Oh, Jesus wasn't ready for him to come home. He has something to do here!' The doctor said he was alive but might not ever have his mind back—that he had been gone too long without blood pressure.

"Well, he came back in every way. He knew the Lord had saved him and he loved the Lord from then on.

"Another incident occurred when he'd gone to the hospital another of his many times there. He had a very bad attack and was in great danger but it passed. When I went to the room a nurse assigned to another patient was standing there. (There were two intensive-care rooms together, all glass, so as to observe the patients at all times.) She told me that something amazing had happened. I said I knew—he was really bad. But she said, 'No, you don't know! I saw something and I don't know why I was allowed to see, but I saw it!' She then began to explain that she was there with her patient and became aware of activity in Earl's room. He was in a bad way—calling out to God—and suddenly she saw angels all around. The room was bright with them! Each time he would call out 'God help me,' the angels would glow brighter and go closer to Earl. The nurses seemed to be in a state of panic and didn't know what to do for immediate aid. As Earl called out (and also seemed in a panic), the angels got brighter and Earl calmed down and began telling the *nurses* what to do for him to help him. It worked and he got through the attack and was fine."

These are the angels we seek. They are always at the ready but are allowed to intervene as far as we are deserving and in contact with them and as long as it is within God's Plan.

They respond to prayers like beacons of light that draw them down. They wait for us to implore them.

"I never knew how intricately balanced and cared for our lives are," said a near-death researcher about the constant involvement of good spirits who honor us when we are devout, when we tend to Christian duty, when we honor God.

"I love churches: they are full of angels," says an alleged Irish mystic. "There might only be a few people in church, but there is always a great hustle and bustle among the angels there. People don't realize how many angels there are in a church; the angels are there praising God and waiting for God's people to come and join them, but frequently no one does. At Mass on a Sunday the place is packed with angels: guardian angels with every person, angels standing around the priest at the altar, and lots more angels which God sends down." At a monastery, she saw monks shining brightly because they were so clean, "not just in their bodies, but in their souls, too. They prayed as they worked and I noticed the angels were praying with them." When she goes past a graveyard, she said, "I always see angels there. If there is a funeral going on it will be full of angels but even if there is just a single person there, they will be surrounded by angels giving them the comfort they require." She saw the Archangel Michael as "so bright it was as if you could see for miles and miles inside of them; as if you were going down a long, long road; as if you were passing through time itself." They dress according to their mission. An atheist who had a brush with death said that when he saw angels in their full glory "it was almost unbearable. The brightness of the light that radiates from them is brighter than the light from a welding torch. Their light doesn't burn the eye, but it is frightening because it is so different from our experience of life. Brighter than lightning, beautiful beyond comparison, powerful, loving, and gentle are words that fail to describe them." He said no artist (and he was one) could paint them. "How do you describe love on a canvas?" he commented. "Our angels are ever vigilant to protect us from evil that originates from other dimensions of the unknown universes. We don't have to worry about it. We should just be glad they are there keeping us safe. There exist supernatural beings that seek chaos. They have no power over us except the power we give them. They are known as demons, the devil, or evil spirits. They should be rejected as much as possible. The power of God and the power of God's angels is much greater than they are. The best defense against evil is to be filled with the Holy Spirit."

Let us repeat this: the best defense is an infilling with the Holy Spirit.

Said the Irish seer: "All babies see angels and spirits, but at about the time a child starts to talk they begin to be told what's real and what's not real, and so if things are not solid like their toys, then they are only pretend. Young children are conditioned and lose the ability to see and experience more. Because education starts earlier nowadays, fewer people are talking to angels."

Usually, the angels function unnoticed—although there are times they leave "calling cards." In Long County, Georgia, a family discovered the image of an angel on a granite slab at a cemetery.

White, blue, pink: angels are of many levels of color and brightness. Their brightness encompasses us with a sense that no matter what, everything is okay and always was.

Be natural.

Let His grace flow.

Purity in full.

More than anything, focus on the afterlife.

Forget not ancestry.

Some who clinically die say that when they were on the other side, they learned the importance of genealogy.

Might it be that there is a connection—and a mission—that involves ancestors? Is this why the New Testament even starts with the ancestry of Jesus?

One man who "returned" says he saw members of his family line as "golden links" joined to form long chains. "Single links weren't as high nor shone as brilliantly as those that were linked together," he remarked. "The more links that were joined, the higher in the air they were and the brighter they shone. The long gold chains were very high, and their combined light made the sun pale in comparison."

In other words, lines of ancestry grow in brilliance as they ascend together toward God.

The Blessed Mother is the new "Eve" and has the chore of helping us strive to be as pure—as immaculate—as she and her family were. Might it be that we are called to rectify wrong inclinations that may go all the way back to Adam (and that "hiss")?

It is, of course, the highest form of speculation. We can say it is important to purify our family lines so that darkness is not passed to future generations (at the same time that we take care not to overly attach to anyone). Whether through learned behavior, genes, or spiritual factors, unfortunate habits, illness, and misfortunes can plague a lineage.

The spirit we need around us is the Holy Spirit, who comes not in a ruckus but with softness. Take it from Rick Sims, who encountered a problem when he moved to Boca Raton, Florida.

"The very first night I was in bed, just about asleep and suddenly I felt paralyzed," he wrote us. "Someone or something landed on top of me pressing me into the mattress. I could not move at all, and was afraid to open my eyes. I tried to say Jesus but again everything was paralyzed. Over and over I tried to say Jesus but my voice was slurred, it sounded like something you see in the movies when a voice is in super slow motion. Finally I was able to say Jesus, and as soon as I did I was free. I opened my eyes and saw a light on in the room; nothing else was there. The next day I called my mom and told her the story. She advised me to say a prayer and ask the Blessed Mother to protect me. So of course I asked her to stay with me the next night, and wouldn't you know, I had one of the best night's sleep I can ever remember."

As for the other side, a woman from Maryland who glimpsed it said, "Suddenly I felt something on both sides of me, not as we might describe a physical touch, but more as a feeling, a sensation of presence—of entities. I could see their light as forms of energy, and I realized that they were angelic beings: loving, pure, holy, helpful. They were assisting me, and I felt a movement upward. Then everything was blue and suspended in the ocean of blue like stardust were golden streams of light that began to pour through me. The light felt so good. If I harbored any lingering heaviness from my life on earth, I knew it was being taken away. And as the radiation continued, I realized there was no longer any sense of gravity, a feeling of being ethereal, with no pulls from the past. Then, like a sweet elixir, the shining rays infusing me washed into the surface a lifetime of memories."

This is what we all must train our eyes upon: the Light at the end of the tunnel.

Anything else diverts us.

We can know that God creates nothing without a purpose and usually that purpose is beyond what our theologians can comprehend—and beyond what anyone can rationalize.

It is only on the other side that these realities will coalesce.

We begin to live Heaven on earth when we aim for joy and live each moment as if it could be our last. "Remember, pray without ceasing," a woman who also experienced death says she was told by angels. "Play, love, laugh, live for the joy of it. Have fun. Happiness is holy."

And holiness makes us happy.

So we have a key life lesson: joy. A boy who had many experiences with angels as he was dying related Heaven to his doctor as "like earth, but we finally get to live our lives without worry and have everything we want." He said angels granted him glimpses of paradise and that it is like "every day is your birthday."

We hear much about peace—how a feeling of well-being and tranquility serves as a marker of spiritual progress. To this we can add happiness. Joy is a sign that we are on the right path. Live it now. Taste Heaven while on earth! Christ is "joy to the world."

Find joy now. To have it is to love without condition. Know this: everyone and everything in life is a test of love. That neighbor or relative who irritates you and deserves rebuke is there to test your willingness to love without condition—to transcend irritations that will seem so very minor afterwards. Live jubilation instead of irritation!

To have joy is to rid anger.

Are you as humble as you think? It is your shield of protection. Be warm. Be righteous. Be sincere. It is to remain away from all extremes. Speak well of others. Do nothing to excess. Be neither lazy nor hyper. Tend not to despair or hopelessness. Do not eat, drink, or gamble with compulsion. Discipline is a key to happiness. Depart from this life with no rancor. Forgive all. If there is purgatory, He will send assistance. He loves us all equally (every single person) and watches every single second of our lives! Don't think that after death you can linger and straighten things out (unless God wills it); He has purgatory for that. Always, go to His Light. You need mainly to love Him. When you do, there should be no fear. Perfect love casts that out.

If there are roadblocks in your life, it could be anger. It could be pride. Whatever, it is the wrong path.

Purify. Wait for Heaven.

Get out from under the yoke of worldly obligation. Let the Holy Spirit fill you. When the Holy Spirit comes, there is contentment.

"Blessed is the man who trusts in the Lord, whose hope is the Lord. He is like a tree planted beside the waters that stretches out its roots to the stream: It fears not the heat when it comes, its leaves stay green; in the year of drought it shows no distress, but still bears fruit," says *Jeremiah* (17: 5-10).

"Blessed the man who follows not the counsel of the wicked nor walks in the way of sinners, nor sits in the company of the insolent," adds a responsorial psalm.

Ask the Holy Spirit for the spirit of balance. To have joy is to get rid of jealousy. Envy is wanting what someone else has, and when we are wanting we are not filled with joy. Don't desire what is not intended for you!

To have joy is to halt the race to get more than the next person. That robs both peace and joy. Instead, cooperate. Wish everyone the best. Find joy in their joy!

Are you having trouble being happy? Do you still feel in competition? Do you begrudge others?

If so, you may have to remove pride from your soul.

Remember what it says in Scripture: "God resists the proud."

Watch over everything, but without paranoia. Send love at the first sign of evil. Pray without ceasing and your journey will be remarkable here and hereafter.

Develop humility and be transformed. With humility and love comes the joy that introduces or births us into Heaven, and those birthdays that are without end.

Notes and Acknowledgments

I would like to thank my wife, Lisa, as always, for her excellent counsel and editing and encouragement and love! My thanks to Judy Berlinski for editing and formatting so finely, and to Peter Massari for his cover—splendid as usual. Thanks to my sister Kathleen Jenkins for proof-reading. And to all who have sent me their accounts and who read our website, www.spiritdaily.com.

Many books, personal conversations, interviews, personal experiences, internet searching, and e-mails went into this work, including *Healing the Haunted* and *A Guide to Healing the Family Tree* by Dr. Kenneth McAll; *Whispers of God's Love* by Mitch Finley; the quote from the writer on caution in discerning spirits in the first chapter is from "Seven Kinds of Ghosts" by Brother Ignatius Mary in St. Michael's Scriptorium. The Kessler book is *Visions, Trips, and Crowded Rooms: Who and What You See Before You Die.* I also used *Return from Tomorrow* by Dr. George G. Ritchie; *Evidence of the Afterlife* by Dr. Jeffrey Long; *My Descent into Death*, by Dr. Howard Storm; *Into the Light* and *Learning from the Light* by Dr. John Lerma; *Angels in My*

Hair, by Lorna Byrne; Betty Eadie's *Embraced by the Light*; and the fascinating nursing website, www.allnurses.com. Also useful as background: Dr. Raymond Moody's *Life After Life* (1975), which coined the term "near-death experience" and was followed by his *Reflections on Life After Life* and *The Light Beyond*. For deathbed visions see *At the Hour of Death*, by Dr. Karlis Osis and Dr. Erlendur Haraldsson.

Many books were used in researching this work, books by sincere people and often medical professionals although often I do not subscribe to their religious views or perspectives, which often stray into psychic or New Age realms. Caution and prayer are greatly advised, as there is deception here as there is among alleged Marian apparitions. As with all such books, we often recommend discernment, for the near-death field can even head into realms of reincarnation or mediumistic phenomena, which we find highly inadvisable (along with any other means of "communicating" with the dead). In following Scripture, we test the spirits, and take what is good, and leave the rest; no spirit that does not confess Jesus as Savior is legitimate. Any that take us away from Christianity are at least partially suspect. See also *An Unpublished Manuscript on Purgatory* (available at www.spiritdaily.com, as are my books *The Other Side* and *After Life*).

About the author

A former investigative reporter, Michael H. Brown, 58, is the author of more than twenty books, most of them Catholic. He has appeared on numerous TV and radio shows, and contributed to publications from *Reader's Digest* to *The Atlantic Monthly*. He is the author of the Catholic bestsellers *The Final Hour*, *The God of Miracles*, and *The Other Side*, and lives in Palm Coast, Florida, with wife Lisa and three children. He is also director of the Catholic news website, Spirit Daily (www.spiritdaily.com).

Other Books by Michael H. Brown

Available at www.spiritdaily.com

THE OTHER SIDE

AFTER LIFE (Heaven, Hell, and Purgatory)

TOWER OF LIGHT (current prophecy)

THE GOD OF MIRACLES (real cases of answered prayers)

SENT TO EARTH: God and the Return of Ancient Disasters

SEVEN DAYS WITH MARY (devotional prayers)

SECRETS OF THE EUCHARIST

THE FINAL HOUR (the Blessed Mother's apparitions)

THE SEVEN